Proceedings of the Second Workshop on
Human Response to Aviation Noise in Protected Natural Areas

Volpe National Transportation Systems Center

Cambridge, MA

May 26-29, 2009

Table of Contents

1. Introduction

Congress passed the National Parks Air Tour Management Act of 2000 (NPATMA) to regulate commercial air tour operations over units of the National Park System[1]. The Federal Aviation Administration (FAA) and the National Park Service (NPS) are jointly developing the Air Tour Management Plans (ATMP) required by this Act, with support from the U.S. Department of Transportation, John A. Volpe National Transportation Systems Center (Volpe Center). Approximately 100 park units will require an ATMP.

Due to the agency overlap of responsibilities inherent in the ATMP process, the FAA and NPS share an interest to develop mutually agreeable and scientifically defensible methods to quantitatively assess aviation noise impacts in National Parks. Although the agencies could pursue wholly independent research programs, public investment in research will realize the highest return if the FAA and NPS jointly develop a prioritized list of research topics and a coordinated strategy for stimulating this research. To this end, the FAA, Western Pacific Region, Office of Special Programs, with assistance from the FAA, Office of Environment and Energy, and the NPS Natural Sounds Program Office, sponsored a research-needs workshop, organized and hosted by the Volpe Center, in October, 2008. Further details on the October workshop can be obtained in the proceedings document[2]. Due to the complexities of the subject matter, a second workshop was required to fully vet the research needs and develop a comprehensive plan. The second workshop, the subject of this document, was organized by and held at the Volpe Center in May, 2009.

These workshops served as a forum for experts in the fields of engineering acoustics, social science, psychology, and recreation management to:

- Exchange information and individual ideas on human responses to aviation noise;
- Identify and discuss uncertainties about the physical and psychological factors that influence aviation noise;
- Identify and discuss uncertainties about acoustic metrics to characterize noise exposure; and
- Discuss the best methods to address these uncertainties

The participants at these workshops were not brought together to form an official Federal Advisory Committee; the ideas and opinions presented were those of the individual participants. The FAA will present the workshop information to the Research and Engineering Development Advisory Committee (REDAC), to seek formal advice on moving forward with new research. The goal of the workshop was to develop a series of steps to guide this new research.

2. Participants

Technical Experts:
Grant Anderson, Independent Consultant
James Fields, PhD, Independent Consultant
Richard Horonjeff, Independent Consultant
Steve Lawson, PhD, Resource Systems Group
Britton Mace, PhD, Southern Utah University (via phone)
Robert Manning, PhD, University of Vermont
Nicholas Miller, HMMH Inc.

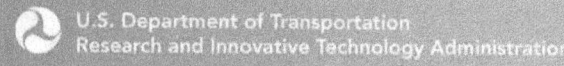

Peter Newman, PhD, Colorado State University

FAA Representatives:
Raquel Girvin, PhD, Office of Environment and Energy, Headquarters
Bill He, PhD, Office of Environment and Energy, Headquarters

NPS Representatives:
Kurt Fristrup, PhD, Natural Sounds Program Office, Ft. Collins
Frank Turina, Natural Sounds Program Office, Ft. Collins

Volpe Center Representatives:
Cynthia Lee
Kristin Lewis
Christopher Roof
Amanda Rapoza, Workshop Organizer
Adam Klauber, Gina Barberio, Note-Takers

3. Discussion Themes

These proceedings organize the information discussed at the workshop into five categories, or discussion themes. The themes are inherently overlapping. To provide a clear summary, however, they are presented individually. A full account of the meeting was documented in a minutes, reproduced in Appendix A.

Research Paradigm
This discussion theme included definitional issues (i.e., arriving at a common definition of noise exposure-response), the goals for and intended uses of the noise exposure-response research, and policy/park management considerations – in particular, criteria and standards by which to establish acceptable noise thresholds (and questions about whether setting absolute standards is desirable).

Survey Development and Research Methods
This discussion theme covered issues of survey design, variables of interest, and data quality.

Sampling and Data Analysis
Closely related to survey research methods are issues of sample size, data analysis, and minimization of uncertainty.

Site Selection
The types of sites to use for research, and how to prioritize among potential sites, were among the issues within this theme.

Measurement Issues
This theme included issues related to acoustic measurement (e.g., accurately establishing aircraft locations), as well as to measuring visitor responses (e.g., when to administer surveys to long-term park visitors).

3.1. Research Paradigm

Workshop participants identified and discussed a range of "foundational" questions about the goals of the research, the kinds of information the research is intended to produce, and the ways in which the research results can help inform park management decisions.

3.1.1. Research Goals

As defined by some researchers, the end goal of the research is a noise exposure-response relationship, expressed as a regression equation, relating a specific visitor response to a quantitative metric of the visitor's noise exposure. With such an equation, it is possible to "plug in" the expected noise exposure and the mediator values (such as site-type), to get an expected visitor response and its statistical uncertainty. This can be classified as a strict interpretation of "dose-response," wherein every measured stimulus (dose) generates a single response data point; researchers analyze data at the most disaggregated level. Alternately, the responses can be analyzed aggregately – by calculating a mean response value (or norm) at set values of dose (or a range of values, often called bins). For example, some studies have generated acceptability curves, based on responses to a series of audio clips with varying natural and aircraft noises (rated on a scale of -4, unacceptable, to +4, very acceptable).[*]

Others ask whether such a purely functional goal might be too narrow. They suggest that the objective should be to create a method, or a set of methods, by which to understand the relationship between visitor experiences and aircraft noise exposure. To begin with, the concept of "response," rather than being seen as unitary, can instead be viewed as a broad approach to thinking about the impact of aircraft noise in a park environment. Considerations include the effects on a variety of park experiences, and the range of ways to characterize the visitors' response to noise (including annoyance, and interference with enjoyment of the park). One workshop participant characterized the strict approaches as "brand name" and the broad concept as "generic" dose response.

A researcher's choice of one approach versus the other often depends on the kinds of park management or policy questions he or she is trying to answer, in addition to analytical considerations. For example, when the research includes stimuli that are likely to be perceived favorably (e.g., natural sounds), as well as stimuli that may be perceived negatively (i.e., aircraft noise), a bi-polar scale with normative analysis may be necessary. In such cases, calculating mean response values makes the results easier to interpret: anything below zero indicates a negative response, while values greater than zero indicate positive responses.

From a management perspective, an important issue is that ultimately, the end goal for the research is to set noise standards/thresholds for the parks – that is, to be prescriptive rather than just descriptive. If a prescriptive role is envisioned, the question becomes selecting an appropriate basis for whatever thresholds are developed.[†] Such bases could be a functional noise exposure-response curve or the acceptability curves documented in Soundscape studies. Workshop participants noted

---

[*] One workshop participant noted that any 9-point bipolar response scale could generate a similar mid-point that is analogous to the point located on an acceptability curve. The point of "acceptability" is just the arithmetic mean of the diverse response scores.

[†] Each park need not have a single noise threshold. Instead, a range of prescriptive information could be provided to a park, to inform a range of possible management actions.

that a threshold-based approach would be consistent with the framework defined in the *Visitor Experience and Resource Protection* (VERP) guidelines[3], which discusses selecting indicators and setting standards to address visitor use management and carrying capacity issues in the National Parks.[*]

Consideration of impact thresholds is made additionally complex by the fact that public policy seeks to balance two sets of considerations. On the one hand, the NPS is primarily interested in providing a positive visitor experience, and desires a graduated noise impact scale that can be applied flexibly and serve as the basis for negotiation with air tour operators. A noise level that does not detract from the visitor experience in one park context might be deemed too loud in another. The FAA, on the other hand, seeks a single, consistent, "impact / no impact" threshold that could be applied uniformly at all parks.

3.1.2.   Context

Another foundational issue, which affects both measurement of noise exposure-response relationships and park management decisions with regard to aircraft noise, concerns the types of sites chosen for study. Previous noise exposure-response noise studies have focused on sites loosely defines as short hikes and overlooks, but there are many other ways in which visitors experience the parks. It is important to understand whether the context of a visitor's park experience mediates his or her response to aircraft noise (a detailed discussion of site context can be found in Section 3.4). Workshop participants noted that previous studies included a relatively limited set of mediators, and it would be beneficial for new studies include a greater range of variables.

3.1.3.   Tools for Park Management

Workshop participants noted and discussed and detail the end goal of the noise exposure-response research: a scientific tool to help enable NPS and FAA manage the airspace over parks cooperatively. Participants agreed that the ideal scientific tool for the research effort to produce would be a spreadsheet-based tool for use by park managers. Such a tool would incorporate the mathematical noise exposure-response relationship(s), and would be customizable to account for the unique characteristics and context of each park, and/or each site within a park. This could, potentially, obviate the need to do a tailored noise exposure-response study at each park and/or site to determine visitor experience impact. Also, such an analysis tool (and the research behind it) would be useful for periodic stakeholder meetings (with the public or inter-agency), to get all participants up to speed on the latest information on noise impacts.

Workshop participants raised several questions related to the incorporation of the noise exposure-response research results into Air Tour Management Plans (ATMPs). Several ATMPs for major parks are currently in development, and are likely to be completed before the noise exposure-response research is concluded. Participants' questions included the following:

- If the ATMPs for parks with significant air tour activity are completed now, will the subsequent noise exposure-response research therefore only influence subsequent ATMPs for less-problematic parks?

---

[*] These indicators and standards can be based on a number of sources, including review of scientific literature, new in-the-field research, consultation with the public, and management judgment.

- Once the noise exposure-response research is completed, will it be possible to update published ATMPs to incorporate the findings? Will doing so generate excessive opposition from air tour operators, who may feel as though FAA and NPS are "changing the rules" retroactively? This issue is particularly acute for the Grand Canyon ATMP (EIS?).

Because of questions like these, workshop participants agreed that producing solid research results as soon as possible is important, and recognized that those results would necessarily be more narrowly focused than what the research effort as a whole will ultimately yield. For example, if initial results do not include data from a wide variety of sites (e.g., if they exclude backcountry sites), they could still be helpful in, for example, defining upper boundaries of annoyance and other responses to noise. There was consensus among the workshop participants that it would be helpful to identify a small set of high-priority areas on which to focus the initial research.

3.2. Survey Research Methods

3.2.1. Survey Questionnaire Development

Deciding what questions to ask the visitor, and how to phrase those questions, is central to the development of an accurate, non-biased survey instrument. With respect to survey question development for the noise exposure-response research, several factors are important. First, survey questions need to measure actual park visitor experiences, rather than respondents' tendency to give positive answers about an experience that should be, and that they had hoped would be, enjoyable. This issue, known as "cognitive dissonance," is common in survey research, but may be exacerbated in park surveys. Given all the time, travel, money and effort often expended to get to a particular site, park visitors may have an incentive to believe the experience was more enjoyable/positive than it actually was. This can lead to respondents ignoring, forgetting, or downplaying negative aspects, such as aircraft noise. [*]

The challenge for researchers is to develop survey questions and/or response scales that cut through the cognitive dissonance to get at the objective truth. One possibility is to ask pointed, specific questions about whether aircraft noise degraded a visitor's experience. The risk, of course, is that such questions can introduce bias (see discussion of cueing, below). Similarly, questions that attempt to measure respondents' attitudes about the "acceptability" or "appropriateness" of aircraft noise in a park setting are potentially valuable, but risk interjecting a normative standard into the survey. An underlying issue concerns evaluating the extent to which respondents understand, and value, concepts such as "natural quiet," and "solitude." Respondents' attitudes about these concepts, although difficult to measure empirically, are important because they may mediate respondents' reactions to noise.

Another important potential source of survey bias is unintended cueing of respondents. This can occur when a park visitor knows he is part of a survey, and as a result is more attuned to aircraft noise during the visit. Cueing can also happen with respondents who were not aware of the survey during their park visit, but who become aware of the context when they are asked to participate in the survey. To a certain extent, informing respondents about the context of a survey is unavoidable, and may be desirable if it helps them focus their attention on the survey topic. As one workshop participant stated, "we have to ask about aircraft noise specifically to know if it is an issue." Nevertheless, highly specific questions carry an inherent risk of cueing bias. For example, a question

---

[*] Involving environmental psychologists in the development of survey questions can help minimize cognitive dissonance.

such as "To what extent does aircraft noise interfere with your sleep?" could bias responses.[*] An alternative approach is to ask more general questions about the visitor's experience, such as "what is your quality of sleep?" and then to correlate that response to sound level data recorded during the time the respondent was in the park. The challenge with this alternative approach is to control for all the factors other than aircraft noise that could also affect the visitor's experience. An analogous issue concerns the use of negative questions (e.g., "to what extent did aircraft noise interfere with your enjoyment of the park?") versus questions that ask for a general assessment of the park's soundscape, with response categories ranging from positive to negative. To address possible cueing/bias issues, one workshop participant suggested a survey design that begins with general questions about the visitor experience, and moves on to more specific questions about annoyance, noise and aircraft.

In summary, workshop participants discussed three survey design approaches to address the cueing issue:[†]

1. Use exclusively cued questions – that is, questions focusing specifically on aircraft noise

2. Combine general "visitor experience" questions with some cued questions

3. Use entirely non-cued questions that ask about the visitor experience generally.

Workshop participants noted that it will be important for future studies to retain the core questions from the original questionnaires, so that any new results relate to prior work and, when combined with previous findings form a coherent data set. This will be particularly important to bring consistency and comparability to longitudinal studies, in which the same (or similar) sites are surveyed at different points in time (e.g., 10 years later). In addition, using questions from prior studies that received OMB approval may help insure OMB approval of the new (proposed) surveys.[‡]

Participants noted two prior questions, in particular, as being essential to carry forward (notwithstanding the possible cueing issues mentioned above):

1. "Were you bothered or annoyed by aircraft noise during your visit to this site?"

2. "How much did sound from aircraft interfere with your appreciation of the natural quiet and sounds of nature at this site?"

3.2.2. Potential New Variables

Workshop participants had a detailed discussion about the types of variables to include in analyses, and the process by which to refine the choice of noise exposure, response, and mediator variables. There was recognition that if NPS is going to manage aircraft noise in places where noise exposure-response survey research has not been performed, information on specific aspects of the site which influence the visitors' response to aircraft noise will be required. Consequently, noise exposure response research analyses, intended to yield generalizable models should, ideally, include the same kinds of indicators and information as park managers have access to for their sites.[§] This means

---

[*] Air tour operators have argued that park aircraft noise surveys have produced biased results because of cueing.

[†] Survey pretesting can help researchers select the best approach.

[‡] A participant noted that this is not always the case. In one instance, OMB disallowed a question on a survey although it had been administered previously to 80,000 respondents successfully.

[§] One workshop participant stated, "If the NPS managers have supplied data on 15 site characteristics that they are selecting for and we can only examine 13 . . . there is a problem."

potentially adding additional variables; it does not mean dropping any existing noise exposure or response variables. That is, future studies should be consistent with the "core" of past studies in terms of the noise exposure and response variables studied, the scales used (e.g., bi-polar versus uni-polar), and the mediator variables included, particularly mediators that are applicable to a wide range of sites. In addition, future studies could, potentially, add new noise exposure and response variables, and mediator variables relevant to new types of sites. Among the potential mediator variables discussed were the following:

- Those found to be significant in past studies:

  - Group status of respondent (i.e., alone, or part of a group)

  - Gender of respondent

  - Presence of children with respondent

  - Whether this is the respondent's first visit to the park.

  - Duration of park visit. —This is a possible mediator because a park visitor may become aware of the sound components of the park (such as natural quiet) over the course of a visit, and also because the visitor's initial expectations about sound levels in the park may change over the course of a visit. Often, the appreciation for the soundscape or natural quiet in a park is a momentary concern. Therefore, the key question for park visitors may be, is it important at any moment in time to be able to access the natural quiet?

  - How many aircraft the respondent heard. Asking this question is really a way of gauging the respondent's level of awareness about aircraft.

  - Presence of signage about air tour flights. In at least two previous studies (White Sands and Denali), it is likely that signage caused visitors to adjust their expectations about natural quiet, and may have affected their levels of annoyance with aircraft noise

For future studies, workshop participants gave special consideration to one particular potential mediator: crowding. The level of crowding at a site could influence responses to noise, but this relationship has not been investigated previously. For example, prior studies did not count the number of people who were skipped during interviewing, and therefore did not have a measure of total visitors.

Crowding – defined as visitor density by time – can be tracked directly by observation or automatic (such as infra-red) counters, or indirectly via data on the number of permits issued or entrance fees collected each day. There are several potentially important dimensions to crowding. First is the distinction between the absolute number of people, and the existence of groups. People traveling in a group with friends or relatives may have a qualitatively different experience with respect to crowding than they would if they were among the same number of strangers. The next dimension is the amount of time and/or distance separating visitors. Perceptions of crowding may increase as temporal and spatial separation decrease; research could quantify this relationship, and reveal whether minimum separation thresholds exist. The final dimension of crowding is the potential for "temporal displacement" of survey responses. This label simply refers to the possibility that in a crowd of visitors who arrived at various times, some survey respondents may inaccurately recall the times at which noise events occurred, erroneously displacing the events either forward or backward in time. For this reason, it may be judicious for researchers to try to identify when respondents arrived at a given site.

Crowding is fundamentally a subjective concept: different respondents will perceive the same density of people in different ways, and may, furthermore, have different annoyance thresholds with respect to crowding. Therefore, noise exposure-response studies wanting to include crowding as a potential mediator would ideally measure visitor density objectively, and ask respondents subjective questions to measure their perceptions and attitudes. One workshop participant observed that the research literature on crowding includes a great deal of information on mediators, many of which may be applicable to noise research.

The workshop participants noted that it will be important, in future studies, to solicit input from park managers regarding mediator variables to include. However, rather than asking park managers for a 'laundry list" of mediators (doing so could generate an untenably long list), researchers could instead present a short list of potential variables to park managers for input and feedback. In order to include new mediator variables, it may be necessary to eliminate some mediators that were used previously. Prior mediators that were not statistically significant could be dropped.

3.3. Data Analysis and Sampling

While new studies are being planned, existing data from past studies can be further mined. Workshop participants discussed a three-step approach to re-analyzing current data sets.

1) First, initial regression analyses using a sub-set of responses (typically annoyance and interference with natural quiet), selected a priori, would identify the individual independent variables (noise exposure 'dose' descriptors, further discussed in Section 3.3.1) and mediator variables that offer reasonably good predictive power. Multiple model specifications could be developed in this way.

2) In the second step, more detailed regression analyses would test various augmentations of the noise exposure descriptors. For example, the "percent time aircraft are audible" (%TA) variable could be augmented by combining it with a measure of the sound level during those times (such as equivalent sound level (L_{eq})) – in this way, a composite noise exposure variable could be computed. This second step would focus on improving the fit of the models (i.e., reducing standard error and tightening confidence intervals), and would help identify predictor variables that could be excluded from the analysis.

3) The third step would seek to improve the fit of the models further by adding mitigating variables, and would cross-validate the model results by site (cross-validation and its associated methodological issues are discussed below). Among the potential mitigating variables suggested were the duration of the visit to a particular site, and the type of site.[*]

The underlying aim of the three-step process would be to specify regression models that use the smallest number of explanatory variables to yield good regression coefficients, while also minimizing the uncertainty of the results. As one workshop participant noted, the goal should not be to find the "best" predictor, but rather to determine which predictors can be excluded from the models without compromising the results. It was noted that lack of data for some sites may negatively affect the predictive ability of any given model specification.

It was noted that existing data should be analyzed to see if there is large response variation between different sites within each category (e.g., between the various overlook sites). If this is the case, it may indicate there are factors other than aircraft noise influencing the results. It will be important to identify

---

[*] The former is a continuous variable; the latter would need to be coded as a categorical variable. Alternatively, a series of dummy variables could be developed to code the different site types.

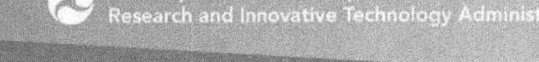

the variables other than noise exposure that are most powerfully associated with the variation between sites, so that these can be tested for/accounted for in future studies.

3.3.1. Noise Exposure Descriptor / Summary Variables

There is reason to believe that much of the variance in past noise exposure-response models stems from the fact that current noise exposure descriptors do not adequately account for many of the aspects of a visitor's noise exposure. Aspects of this exposure include the maximum level, average level, relative level, duration, and duration of natural quiet between exposures. Participants noted that it would be useful to determine if combinations of existing summary metrics provide better predictive power that a single summary metric alone. Previous studies have rejected this notion, but not conclusively. In the future, acoustic data can and should be collected with spectral information (not just A-weighted sound levels, as in the current database), and analyzed to determine if the inclusion of spectral information will yield better results.

In addition, ambient sound levels may mask aircraft noise, and/or mediate visitor responses to aircraft noise. It will be beneficial to know the ambient sound levels at study sites, in order to subtract them from the total sound levels during noise events, or to statistically control for their effects in the regression models.

However, many participants and the agencies noted that, unless new descriptors yield significantly better results, the ease of use (both in communication to stakeholders and in computer simulations) may outweigh the potential benefits of descriptors which offer only minor improvement.

3.3.2. Uncertainty

Workshop participants engaged in a detailed discussion of the factors affecting the uncertainty of regression results – typically depicted as an "uncertainty region" surrounding noise exposure-response curves reflecting variance not explained by the regression models.

Perhaps the most important factor with respect to uncertainty is data quantity (i.e., sample size), particularly for different types of sites. Visitors and sites exhibit variability – this is normal and desirable. At any given site, visitor variability tends to average out given a sufficiently large random sample of visitors. Because noise exposure-response studies are typically carried out one site at a time, however, site variability does not average out, causing the uncertainty regions around the curve to expand greatly due to variability among sites that is not explained by the regression coefficients. Future studies should work to correct this deficiency. The goal, as one workshop participant stated, is to measure "lots of visitors, at lots of sites."[*] More specifically, the challenge is balancing the number of sites studied against the number of visitors surveyed per site.

With respect to the issue of variability, one participant observed that trying to study differences between parks would be extremely difficult (i.e., effectively characterizing each entire park) and would require enormous resources (i.e., the need to study many parks). It may be better to focus on understanding variability between sites within parks. For example, new research could examine backcountry sites in parks where prior studies have examined front country sites. As this participant stated, "if we try to understand park-to-park differences, we are opening up a Pandora's box that would require substantial additional research."

---

[*] Scenic overlook sites have been well represented in prior studies, but back-country sites have not.

As discussed above, augmenting noise exposure variables can help improve the fit of the regression models and reduce uncertainty. This can be particularly helpful when trying to minimize the uncertainty associated with the variability of noise exposure data from different sites. Well-chosen noise exposure augmentations can help fit different noise exposure characteristics from different sites into a single, "unified" noise exposure-response regression model that is applicable across sites.

Insufficient data for certain noise exposure levels (however level is defined) can also contribute to uncertainty. Noise exposure-response graphs (with noise exposure level along the X axis) often exhibit "hourglass" shaped uncertainty regions: they are wide at low noise exposure levels, narrow considerably toward the middle of the noise exposure range, and then widen again at high noise exposure levels. This is a symptom of a lack of noise exposure data at the high and low ends of the range.

Another factor that can increase the uncertainty of noise exposure-response regression results is the choice of noise exposure scale. Different scales will produce different noise exposure-response curve shapes, and hence different regression results. This is particularly apparent when a logarithmic noise exposure scale is used rather than a linear one. Some shapes are a better fit than others; researchers need to select noise exposure scales carefully, based on theoretical and methodological criteria.

Another factor contributing to predictive uncertainty of noise exposure-response regression models is the practice of cross-validation. This is a widely-used technique for assessing the accuracy of a predictive statistical model – that is, how well the model will work given an independent data set. Cross-validation is particularly useful in cases where collecting additional data would be costly, difficult, or dangerous. Generically, the practice involves partitioning the data into sub-sets, estimating the model using one sub-set, and validating it against the other(s). In the case of noise exposure-response studies, this would mean partitioning the data based on the study sites, excluding one site from the analysis and running the regression calculations again, and then comparing the predicted results of the new regression to the data for the site that was excluded. This process would then be repeated with each of the other sites excluded, one a time, from the analysis. Weighting can be used to adjust for different numbers of respondents in the data sub-sets.

3.3.3. Sample Size

A discussion ensued about developing an optimized sampling plan to achieve this balance. The first issue raised was whether the number of sites should be determined based on the minimum sample size requirements for a statistically valid sample. Clearly, at some level this determination will be important, because it will enable researchers to develop a total cost estimate for the study.

On the other hand, sample-size considerations alone will be insufficient for determining the number of sites needed. Researchers will also need some initial information about each potential site. Some of this information can be obtained from NPS, including the number of annual visitors, the coverage area (square miles), and the number of air tour flights. These existing data could help researchers determine the balance between the number of future sites and the number of visitors surveyed at each site. The underlying issue here is that, during the initial phase, researchers will need to develop estimates of site variability with respect to the factors to of interest. Only then will they be able to determine how many sites they need to include in the study.

3.4. Site Selection

Workshop participants discussed a variety of issues related to the selection of sites for future noise exposure-response studies, beginning with the general topic of the types of sites to select. There was concurrence that prior studies provide sufficient data on overlooks and short hikes; new studies should target backcountry sites, historical/cultural sites (including sites where interpretive talks occur), and specialized sites such as memorials/sacred areas and bird watching sites). Data will be needed from multiple examples of each type of site, and it will be important to understand the distribution of sites among these categories so researchers can decide where to concentrate future efforts. There may be additional sites available within parks that have been studied previously. Similarly, some parks have multiple management zones within them, which could translate to multiple survey zones.

With approximately 90 parks potentially available for study, and perhaps four or five potential sites per park, narrowing the list will be a significant task. Researchers will need guidance from NPS to help them classify sites and develop selection criteria. Site selection could emphasize sites with high visitor use, sites with high air-tour and/or aviation activity, outstanding recreational value (ORV) areas, sites with particular management concerns, and sites whose characteristics can help provide data to fill gaps in the existing knowledge base.[*,†] In addition, stakeholder input and NEPA analyses can be used to select sites for inclusion. Participants also noted the importance of insuring that the selected study sites are consistent with management zones specified in park general management plans and/or NPS management zones. This is not a trivial consideration; a major national park frequently has numerous management schemes within it.

Once an initial site list is developed, researchers will need to evaluate the cost and logistics of studying each site (in terms of both acoustic measurements and visitor surveys), and be prepared to reject certain sites even if they are desirable. To pare the initial list down to a small number of prototype sites, researchers will need to evaluate a number of factors at each site. These include:

- Spatial Character of Visitor Use (concentrated, linear or dispersed). Dispersed sites are particularly challenging for research because noise measurements and visitor surveying must take place across a much larger area, and potential survey participants are harder to locate.[‡] Linear sites (defined by trails or a river) tend to be easier, because park visitors and air tour aircraft may travel in parallel.

- Length of Typical Visit (minutes, hours, single day, multi-day)

- Intensity of Visitation or Crowdedness (high, moderate, low)

- Researcher access to site. (*Drive up*, day hike, *overnight-hike)*

- Number of points of entry for visitors

---

[*] VERP site classifications and/or NPS site designations (e.g., National Scenic Rivers, National Recreation sites, National Historic Parks) could be useful in classifying study sites.

[†] Within the four general site categories, participants identified a number of sub-categories. The workshop ultimately produced the following list: multi-day backcountry, day-hike backcountry, frontcountry-short hike, frontcountry overlook, frontcountry developed, interpretive talk, battlefield (dispersed historic), historic (concentrated), historic (indoor)

[‡] Determining where to take sound measurements at a dispersed site is challenging, particularly because air tour operators are not always willing to discuss their flight routes.

- Difficulty of data acquisition (e.g., distances, difficulty locating respondents, vulnerability to weather)

- Areas shielded from noise (e.g., indoor exhibits)

- Distribution of aircraft overflights (altitudes, spatial, frequency of operation)

- Natural Ambient (High, Moderate, Low, Very Low)

These characteristics were used to build a list of prototypical sites, to guide workshop discussions, summarized in Table 2.

Table 1. Proto-Typical Site Characteristics and Relation to Difficulty of Data Acquisition

Prototype Name	Spatial Character of Visitor Use	Intensity of Visitation	Researcher Access to Study Site	Visitor Points of Entry	Shelter or Shielded Points	Estimated Natural Ambient	Difficulty of Data Acquisition	Assumed Noise Sensitivity / Research Priority
Multi-Day Backcountry	Dispersed	Low	Overnight	Undefined	No	Very Low	Extremely	High
Backcountry Destination / campground	Linear/ Concentrated	Low	Overnight Hike	Many	Maybe	Low	Very	High
Extended Day-Hike	Linear	Moderate	Day-Hike	1 or 2	No	Low	Very	High
Historic/ Cultural	Dispersed	High	Drive-up/ walk	Many	Yes	Moderate	Moderate	High
Interpretive Talk/Activity	Concentrated (around speaker)	High (in groups)	Drive-up/walk	One	Maybe	Moderate	Slightly	High
Front country Campgrounds	Concentrated	High	Drive-up	Many	Yes	Moderate	Slightly	Medium
Front country Short Hike	Linear	Moderate	Short Walk	Few	Yes	Low	Moderate	Low
Front country Destination	Concentrated	High	Drive-up	One	No	Moderate	Slightly	Low
Developed	Concentrated	High	Drive-up	Many	Yes	Moderate	Moderate	Low

Within each particular site, researchers hope for reasonable variability in noise exposure levels, in order to build good noise exposure-response models. Limited exposure variability within sites would necessitate additional sites or a variety of days / seasons at a single site, which would add to the cost and complexity of the research effort. Exposure variability is related to exposure duration: the longer the exposure, the less variation there will be between individuals.[*] The underlying goal at each site is to survey many visitors, who have been exposed to a wide range of noise levels.

---

[*] For example, if aircraft are audible, on average, during 50% of any given day, most day-long visitors would have a

Campgrounds were the subject of a focused discussion among the workshop participants. There was agreement that campgrounds (both front-country and back-country) should be listed as prototype study sites. Campground users may have different noise sensitivities than other types of park visitors. One reason for this potential difference is that much of the time spent at a campground comes after the day's other activities are done. As such, the campground can be place where park visitors reflect on and discuss what they have seen and learned during the day. Another important factor is that camping usually involves evening activities, whereas previous noise exposure –response studies have all occurred during the day. It may be useful to evaluate noise exposure-response relationships in the evening. Also, the possible mediating effect on noise response of proximity to other visitors (aka, crowding) may be different if that proximity occurs at a campground rather than, for example, on a hiking trail. There is an additional set of considerations with respect to backcountry campsites because the users of these campsites may be more sensitive to noise.[*]

3.5.   Measurement Issues

Workshop participants devoted significant attention to the challenges of measuring noise in the park environment and the park visitors' reactions to it. Some of these issues overlap with survey methodology, while others are distinct.

3.5.1.   Noise Exposure Data Collection

Participants discussed three potential approaches for obtaining noise exposure data: direct measurement using fixed sound level measurement devices, direct measurement using portable sound measurement devices, such as a dosimeter, and computer modeling. Workshop participants agreed that it would be useful to conduct detailed tests to compare methods for measuring or estimating noise exposure over wide-areas.

In the case of direct measurement (where researchers go into the field with recording equipment), a significant challenge is that park visitors move around – they flow over a site over a period of time. For this reason, sound measurements should be dynamic across time also, to generate a dynamic noise map. Given the cost and complexity of developing such a map, some studies are doing the next best thing: they are using static noise maps combined with GPS trackers worn by survey participants, so that researchers can pinpoint where on the noise map the participants are at any given time.

Establishing a noise-contour map (even a static one) using direct measurement is challenging for several reasons. First, air traffic may be irregular and dispersed (especially at sites whose physical layout is dispersed rather than linear). Second, both air tour traffic and general aviation traffic need to be recorded, because survey respondents typically do not distinguish between them. Third, pinpointing the location of aircraft at the time the sound measurements are made is difficult. It is possible to do so using photo-triangulation, but that technique is limited to relatively small areas

---

%TA narrowly distributed around 50. However, due to temporal variations during daily activity (e.g., more aircraft fly during the afternoon than morning), hour-long visits might have a variation between 25% and 75%. Similarly, visitors at a site for only 10 minutes may 'just happen' to have aircraft audible 100% of the time, while others will not experience a single aircraft overflight.

[*] From a management perspective the protection of the acoustical environment in the remote backcountry would likely be sufficient to protect these other environments.

(i.e., acres rather than square miles) and requires three simultaneous photographs be taken of each aircraft whose sound is recorded.[*], [†]

Prior to any direct measurement, an on-site scoping visit should always be conducted to assess how people interact with a location. NPS has detailed information on visitation such as time at certain sites and visitor movement in parking lots. Different parks may require different amounts of scoping. For example, a Grand Canyon backcountry assessment may take several days.

As an alternative to direct measurements, noise exposure can be modeled. To do this, existing aircraft models would be validated using measurements made over an extended period of time at fixed locations. These sound levels are plotted using air tour route maps to establish average noise contours and visitor exposure.[‡] Of course, using average sound levels introduces the possibility of statistical error.

Portable measurement devices, such as dosimeters or digital recorders, provide yet another possible means to gather noise data. One workshop participant suggested pilot testing portable sound recorders carried by survey participants. These would record ambient sound as well as episodic noise. Challenges with this approach include asking park visitors to carry another piece of gear (there would be weight issues), the possibility of equipment damage, difficulties distinguishing aircraft noises from ambient sounds (e.g., a loud stream, wind), and the need during the pilot testing to conduct simultaneous direct noise monitoring to verify the accuracy of the dosimeters.

3.5.2.   Sound Source identification

It is essential to be able to distinguish between aircraft and other sound sources in a park. This is particularly important when sound recording is being conducted without field observers (i.e., using automated equipment). Previous hierarchical methods of sound-source logging have been criticized, but new systems can distinguish between different sound sources.[§] Despite these advances, several issues remain. First, without human field observers it is difficult to assess audibility (as opposed to volume). Second, the issues of non-aircraft anthropogenic sources and masking have not been addressed. Workshop participants concurred that studies of live sound-source identification and machine–based sound- sound-source identification should continue.

3.5.3.   Interpretive Talks

Interpretive talks provide researchers with a rare opportunity to directly observe and record noises as the survey participants are exposed to them.[**] It is easy for researchers to monitor ambient sound levels and aircraft noise, to determine whether the latter interferes with the former, and also to monitor responses of the audiences to the noise. Furthermore, because most interpretive talks are short (1/2 hour), researchers could conduct multiple measurements in a single day. Workshop participants agreed that interpretive talks should be listed as a priority site category due to preliminary evidence that noise is a problem, and the relative ease of data collection.

---

[*] For each photograph, the angle of the lens above horizontal and the lens's focal length must be recorded.
[†] Radar tracking of aircraft could establish their locations, but it would be prohibitively expensive
[‡] Parks with Air Tour Management plans have known air tour routes
[§] The method NPS uses differentiates when a sound level is "on" or "off" via continual audio and automated 1/8 octave sensing.
[**] Presently there are no empirical data for interpretive talks, but information from telephone interviews with 20 park rangers indicate that aircraft noise events during interpretive talks can be disruptive.

During an interpretive talk, the sound level of the speaker's voice may be lower for listeners at the back of the audience than for those at the front. Consequently, aircraft noise may disproportionately interfere with the ability of listeners at the back to hear the speaker. Workshop participants discussed whether it will be necessary to account for this differential by recording the sound level of each speaker's voice at the source (i.e., to be able to calculate the actual sound level listeners at different distances from the speaker hear).

3.5.4. Multi-Day Visits

When visitors spend multiple hours or even days at a site, their tolerance to noise can evolve. After a certain point, visitors may stop noticing the noise. This raises questions for park managers and survey researchers. For park managers, the question is: if visitors experience noise during their visit, but by the end of the visit have stopped noticing it and/or do not recall hearing it, is the noise still a concern for the park? For survey researchers, there are two related questions. First, is it important or necessary to measure responses to noise as the noise occurs, or can the survey intercept occur at the end of a visit? Second, should researchers record responses to each noise event, or should they record an average response to a series of events that occur over time? Cognitive research shows that, when recalling past events, people tend to combine a series of discrete events into a single, overall synthesis. Furthermore, that synthesis is almost always positive or "happy."

Workshop participants noted the benefit of being able to study noise response as a function of the duration of a park visit, and/or the amount of time after a noise event. For example, surveys could be conducted at different time intervals after a noise event. They acknowledged, however, that sometimes the logistics of surveying backcountry park visitors make it difficult or impossible to measure noise responses as they occur; therefore, surveys are typically administered at the conclusion of long-duration visits (e.g., at the exit trailhead). Even in cases where is would be possible to administer surveys prior to the conclusion of the visit, there could be problems with survey sample size. Once a given respondent is asked a question, the same person cannot be asked the same question again later on. Therefore, different respondents would need to be found for each set of surveys conducted following a noise event.

Another issue related to long-duration visits is that, as noted previously, the longer the duration of noise exposures, the less variability there will be among the noise exposures different visitors experience. In fact, at any given site there may be no variation in exposure among different multi-day visitors. This presents a significant problem, in that data from surveys of long-duration visitors may not support development of noise exposure-response models. Workshop participants discussed potential ways to address the issue. One possibility is that there may be variation between weekday and weekend aircraft traffic and therefore noise exposure levels. Another, more ambitious, potential approach would be to work with air tour operators (e.g., NPOAG members) to have them fly specific routes and at specific altitudes; this would give researchers much better control of noise exposure levels.

3.5.5. Specialized Activities

There was recognition among workshop participants that certain park activities, like bird watching, may require changes to the surveys and timing of the data collection. Surveys may need to include some specific questions for certain activities and certain testing and accommodations for data gathering for those activities.

3.5.6.   Indoor Impacts

Workshop participants discussed the relative importance of studying the impacts of aircraft noise on indoor environments, such as the historical buildings found at most of the park sites in the eastern U.S. There was consensus that indoor sites are most likely less sensitive to noise impacts than outdoor sites, and should therefore be lower on the research priority list.   Overall, participants concurred that noise exposure-response research needs to focus on sensitive sites and times – this is why research to date has excluded 80 percent of the hours when there is less visitation (i.e., evenings, fall through spring months).

3.5.7.   Laboratory Testing

There was an extended discussion among workshop participants about the efficacy of laboratory studies of noise responses. Laboratory studies may be useful for investigating noise exposure metrics that do not yield useful data in the field, and for exploring correlations between noise exposure metrics in a controlled setting. It was noted that NASA conducted this type of research many years ago, but discontinued the testing because it did not yield much data and it was very expensive. Nevertheless, participants agreed that it is worth additional study to understand whether laboratory research can simulate real-world conditions, and to compare laboratory and field-study results. Participants pointed to the European experience studying rural noise impacts in laboratory settings.

Laboratory studies could pre-test audio clips prior to administering them to participants in the field, and could investigate the effects of crowding on noise response using video and audio.[*] One advantage of laboratory studies is that researchers can manipulate the type, order, combinations, and duration of various auditory and visual stimuli. Workshop participants noted that while laboratory studies provide better control of mediating variables than can be achieved in the field, the lab cannot, of course, recreate the all aspects of the real visitor experience.

Several considerations are important when designing laboratory simulations. These include whether to use full sound recording and binaural headsets (to accurately recreate the soundscape a park visitor experiences), and the duration of audio clips to use.   One workshop participant noted that most aircraft noise events last three to five minutes. To simulate this accurately in the lab means having participants listen to long audio clips, which might limit the number of people willing to participate. On the other hand, laboratory studies could recruit paid participants, who would, presumably, tolerate longer sessions.

Workshop participants also discussed alternatives to laboratory studies that may be more cost effective. These include having participants watch nature films on which aircraft noise has been added to the soundtracks.

4. Research Roadmap

The discussions summarized in Section 3 resulted in general agreement on the fundamental components of the roadmap required to meet the research goals. It was recognized that some components will be higher priority than others, but there are many research needs that, if possible,

---

[*] A workshop participant noted that audio clips were used in the field at Muir Woods. The clips were designed so that researchers knew their acoustic characteristics. The first set of clips was aesthetically constructed based on the sound level at the ear; the next set was parametrically selected using the 1/3 octave band, stepped up in 2 dB sound levels.

should be woven into the immediate efforts. Additionally, it is likely that the specifics of each step in the research process will be affected by experiences gained in previous steps. The fundamental steps of the conceptual roadmap are: 1) data analysis, 2) survey instrument development, 3) meeting of FAA and NPS to discuss status and identify priority of data collection sites, 4) data collection design, 5) data collection and analysis, 6) assessment of results. At the conclusion of the workshop, participants produced a list of research steps. This list can help to inform roadmap implementation by briefly summarizing issues that had been discussed.

1) **Data Analysis**

Objective: To mine as much information from existing exposure-response data to inform future research. To streamline and improve the efficiency of future data collection and processing procedures.

Through analysis of existing exposure-response data:

a) Determine significant combination/combinations of acoustic summary metrics.

b) Examine visitor-specific local ambient as a mediating factor

c) Highlight/Eliminate potential mediators in database (Get context-specific site variables).

Based on this analysis:

d) Develop a statistical tool to determine number of sites/parks/visitors needed for new studies.

e) Present results of 3a to FAA/NPS with recommendations for research direction – conclusions, implications for future, questions raised.

To streamline and improve the efficiency of future data collection and processing:

f) Explore post-processing source Identification

g) Explore machine learning, infinite dose analysis

2) **Survey Development**

Objective: Revise and improve survey, recognizing past problems with survey instrument

a) Develop list of evaluative dimensions / values / experiences / site-mediators (wholesale list) through literature review and/or visitor-type focus groups

b) Develop draft survey instrument for review

c) Present and solicit feedback on list of evaluative dimensions / experiential values / site-mediators / site-characterizations / site proto-types at FAA / NPS stakeholder meeting

To anticipate future survey method problems due to site-context

d) Evaluate direct/indirect questions of visitor experience with/without cueing. Evaluate comparability with previous dose-response survey data

3) **Site Selection**

Objective: To solicit information from NPS to determine areas where there are managements concerns and sites which are research-feasible

a) Develop initial list of campground and interpretive-talk sites for data collection

b) Circulated manager survey for NPS site inventory of needs for noise management information, sound preservation issues

c) Develop Research Plan. Consisting of a synthesis of data re-analysis, focus groups, site-inventory and site-scoping.

d) Convene workgroup to develop project schedule

4) **Methods development**

Objective: To develop the methods required for data collection at logistically complex sites. To develop alternate methods to study the relationship between noise exposure and human response.

a) Comparative test of field-noise exposure collection methods for dispersed/ wide-area sites.

b) Explore issue of when/where/how to survey for multi-day visits. Full visit or segmented visit?

c) Develop Electronic Survey Instrument

d) Explore role of field playback

e) Explore role of laboratory experiments

Noise exposure-Response Research Framework (Workshop Draft)

5. References

1 *National Parks Air Tour Management Act of 2000*, Public Law 106-181, 114, Stat. 61, Title VIII, Section 801 (April 2000).

2 "Proceedings of the Workshop on Human Response to Aviation Noise in Protected Natural Areas", US Department of Transportation , Volpe National Transportation Systems Center, Cambridge, MA, October, 2008. http://www.faa.gov/about/office_org/headquarters_offices/arc/programs/air_tour_management_plan/document s/Proceedings%20DR%20Workshop_Final_03_24_09.pdf

3 The Visitor Experience and Resource Protection (VERP) Framework: A Handbook for Planners and Managers. US Department of the Interior, National Park Service, Denver Service Center, Denver, CO, September, 1997.

 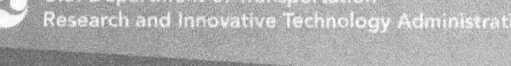

Appendix A

Meeting Minutes

Participants: Cynthia Lee, Amanda Rapoza, Christopher Roof, Raquel Girvin, Peter Newman, Steve Lawson, Jim Fields, Nick Miller, Grant Anderson, Kristin Lewis, Dick Horonjeff, Adam Klauber, Bill He (via phone), Britt Mace (via phone), Frank Turina and Kurt Fristrup joined ~ 2:30pm.

Welcome and Introductions.

<table>
<tr><td>

Purpose

1. Discuss, as individuals, our understanding of human response to aviation noise.
2. Identify the gaps in the 'collective' understanding.
3. Provide views on both short -term and long - term research needs.

</td><td>

This workshop is a forum to exchange information and individual ideas on:

• Uncertainties and gaps in our understanding of the physical and psychological factors which influence human response to aviation noise.
• Uncertainties in our understanding of acoustic metrics which will sufficiently characterize the noise exposure.
• The best methods to address these uncertainties

</td></tr>
</table>

We covered purpose 1 last fall. Now it is time to get down to business and cover steps 2 and 3.

This workshop is not:

A Federal Advisory Committee
• FAA is not asking for a consensus

FAA will present inputs from the workshop to REDAC to seek formal advice on moving forward with the research.

REDAC is the Research and Engineering Development Advisory Committee. A briefing will be provided to FAA regarding proceedings of this workshop – we will consult REDAC to seek formal advice from the research.

• This group seems more configured more for airports than parks.   Maybe question the lack of environmental group representation in REDAC.
• NPOAG (the National Parks Overflights Advisory Group) is another advisory group. The outcomes of this workshop will also be presented to them.

Day 1 Agenda / Goals

✓ Define terminology / review jargon
✓ Explore fundamental assumptions
✓Review available doseresponse data and identify lessons for design of further data collection
[All before lunch!]
✓Discuss research framework
✓Identify characteristics of prototype sites

Goals for the morning are to:

- Review status
- Review terminology and jargon we all use so that we can be sure we're talking the same language,
- Review the current dose-response database, talk about its implications for future research.

After lunch:

- Discuss basic research framework.
   o This framework is certainly not the only way to structure the research.
   o Can discuss if alternate methods would lead us down a better path.
- Discuss how to define the characteristics of prototype sites.

Day 2 Agenda / Goals

Discuss Research Methods
am:
- Identify challenges and propose solutions for data acquisition at each proto-type site

pm:
- Identify need and timing for testing of concepts and/or methods

---

Tomorrow:

- How to collect data at these different types of sites?
- Is there anything besides field testing that can or needs to be done (such as prep work and other research)?

Day 3 Agenda / Goals

am:
- Discuss variables to be collected universally
- Propose research timeline

pm:
- Outline workshop report.
- Discuss next steps

Thursday:

- Discuss what variables to must be collected, to ensure that we have an adequate, universal survey
- Compile views on next steps.

Discussion: What is the end goal of the research effort?

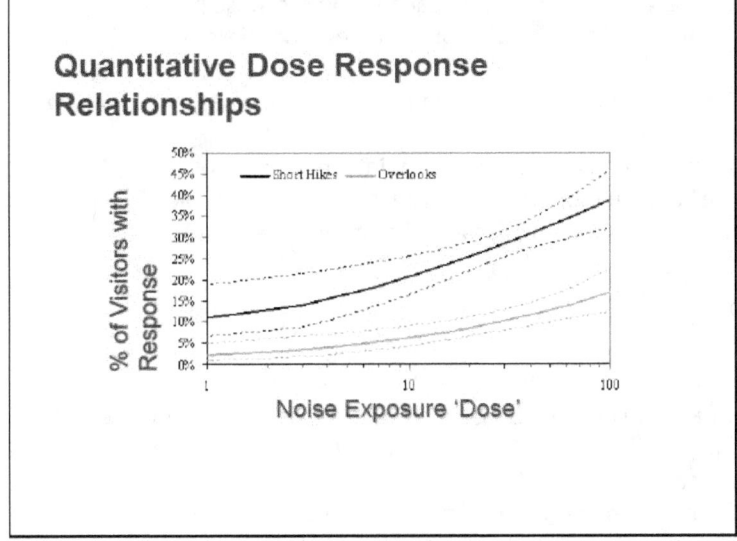

Quantitative Dose Response Relationships

End goal, in the minds of some researchers, is a dose response relationship, where noise dose is the independent variable, and visitor response is the dependent variable. There is a functional relationship between the two.

Comments:

- Maybe the end goal should be broader: To create method/set of methods to understand the relationship between visitors and aircraft noise.
  - Dose-response may mean something different to different individuals.
  - In some cases a norm curve could be substituted.

- Consider the: "response" to include a broad approach to thinking about what the impact is of having aircraft noise in this environment.
  - Includes annoyance and interference with enjoyment
  - Also includes whether the aircraft noise affects any type of experiences in the park.
- Consider more types of sites beyond short hikes and overlooks. We use the term "mediators" and there are other variables. The term "Context" is also used for this concept in some literature and may be useful; the analysis is the same. The use of the term is slightly different.
- The end goal is a dose-response equation – acoustic dose against visitor response, including mediator variables that vary by site and by visitor. Plug in the dose and the mediators; get the expected response and its uncertainty.
- What about the prescriptive aspect? Descriptive is the raw relationship. Prescriptive is how much is too much – at what point would you draw the line for a determining a standard (e.g., for park regulations)? It doesn't have to be a single threshold. You can provide a range of prescriptive information to a park to give a range of possible actions.
- Soundscape studies have used a series of audio clips with varying natural and aircraft noises (rated -4 unacceptable to +4 very acceptable) to generate an "acceptability" curve.
  - Any 9-point bipolar response scale could generate a similar mid-point that is analogous to the point located with an acceptability curve. The point of "acceptability" is just the arithmetic mean of the diverse response scores.

- There is the brand-name dose response and the generic dose response. We are discussing the term dose response and one approach is the brand-name dose-response.
- Let's say it is a "favorability" response. 10% have a normative response that it is okay at this level. If you survey them you find the responses scattered around the normative point
  - How do we handle the dispersion in responses? Should we graph each of the response points on the scale or use an arithmetic mean? We should avoid the use of "norm" to describe these types of questions.
  - The Y-axis is the rating scale, the points are the mean value for each corresponding dose, and anything below the zero scale suggests a negative response.
  - It could include other stimulus that would be viewed favorably. The point when you cross move from a condition that are on average "Acceptable" to condition that are on average "unacceptable"
  - This is simply a discussion of whether you are using a bipolar scale. That is, whether you have a bi-polar scale on your y axis.

Standards and Thresholds are synonymous.

- In VERP there is a reference to particular standards. In dose-response studies, there is an analogous search for "thresholds" in looking for points of inflection.
- In VERP, a standard is an agency decision that is an indicator.
- We are trying to define a visitor-based standard - information to determine the impact on visitors.

Response:

- The dependant variable in our quantitative relationship
- Variable to characterize visitor reaction
- Evaluation of the quality of an experience
- Judgment about the extent to which aircraft noise impacts the an experience.
- A feeling about aircraft noise at a time or location.

DOSE:

- The independent variable in our quantitative relationship
- A numeric representation ('metric') of the salient characteristics of noise exposure:
  1. Sound Level,
  2. Spectral Characteristics,
  3. Duration,
  4. Number of Exposures or Events

- An indicator of visitor experience.

Factors / Mediators

Physical or psychological variables which help to explain the variation in human response.

 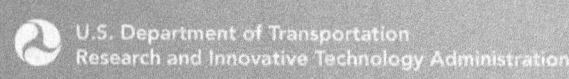

Factors/mediators/context will all influence the outcome.

- Previous analyses only included factors that NPS can manage. New analyses should go beyond this.

Comments:

- We should add more variables (not advocating dropping any). It is useful to keep the variables NPS is using for management. If NPS is going to manage sites that have not been surveyed they will have to use the data available. They will have some other indicators, but not necessarily a survey. We need to have the indicators and information included in our analysis that they will have about the site as a management tool.
- For example, we could use the averages age of visitor at the site. We might be able to use this variable to make predictions about response, but it is not certain that the managers could use age to make similarly accurate predictions given the limited information they have available about a site.

The end goal – a tool

- The idea is that managers could use a spreadsheet, with tailored input about a site, to make management decisions and learn how people react to aircraft noise.
  - We could ask managers about the characteristics of a site and see how the managers' information would predict how the visitors would react at each of the sites.

Two end goals: The end goal of the entire research effort is the agency tool / spreadsheet calculator. The end goal of this workshop is to obtain a series of research steps to move the research forward.

Discussion: Balancing dueling desires: Impact Thresholds vs. Visitor – Experience Standards

- FAA would like to manage impacts; NPS would like to manage for a positive visitor experience.
  - Can we invert dose and instead look at the number of people who are not affected in any way by noise?
  - Inverse or not, too much of the visitor population is affected. NPS may determine that impact is unacceptable.
  - NPS is more interested in how many people are enjoying a positive experience (e.g. "how good was the value of spending time at the location")
  - FAA wants a single threshold, NPS says no – we need a graduated scale. NPS believes there is an impact to management. Tour operators would be concerned because they say that it is never good enough.
  - [NPS] Standards are written to allow for negotiation and flexible implementation. Sometimes, the standards are hard to figure out, as there must be multiple standards - for example for different species.
  - FAA wants "no impact" vs. "impact". NPS seems to accept a process of negotiation. FAA wants a standard and then wants to move on.

Agenda Item: Presentation, Grant Anderson - Lessons from Past Data and the Pending Re-analysis

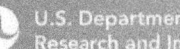
Lessons from Past Data and the Pending Re-analysis

Grant Anderson

Noise Exposure—Human Response Workshop II: 26-28 May 2009

Overview

- Initial lessons from the past
- The pending re-analysis: From data to dose-response
- How to:
  - Obtain decent slopes
  - Obtain narrow uncertainty regions
  - Minimize "unexplained" site variability, including:
    - Cross-validation by site
    - Approximate input during application
- Summary: Main lessons

Initial lessons from the past

- We have enough overlooks (6) and short hikes (7).
- We need other site types (contexts), especially:
  - Backcountry
  - Historical/cultural, including interpretive talks
  - Special cases (memorial/sacred, bird watching).

Future data: For each of these, we need multiple sites

It is not going to be easy to reduce uncertainty for overlooks as we may have to quadruple the number. Instead, we should concentrate on other site types (contexts). Other contexts: near and "true" weeklong backcountry, interpretative/historical talks, special cases (memorial, sacred, bird watching).

Comments:

- If there is significant variation in responses within the current sites for overlooks or short hikes these variations might be overwhelming the dose. If there is enormous between-site variation right now we need to address that.
- What are the most powerful variables that explain this variation between sites? We can have sites classified as needed. This way, we already have noise dose available in our existing variables.

This presentation will suggest methods to reduce the "spread" between findings at different sites. I have in mind a more complete use of the site characteristics.

Comments:

- There may be visitor attitudes that are common, perhaps, within a park but that may not relate to another NPS unit. There are variations within a park, but these may not be as large as between park units.
- We don't know the distribution of sites. We don't know what to concentrate on for future study.
- The distinction between short hike and overlooks was added as an after thought. Researchers pursued the easy locations to gather data. Can we get additional context from surveying at locations we have already conducted studies?
  - Cost has affected the dose/response studies. Overlooks and short hikes have been completely restricted to sites where people don't go into buildings. Other studies may provide data as to what influences responses.
  - We will have trouble getting beyond the question of what the limited number of sites for conducting this research.
  - There are a number of management zones within each park. It is possible to have dose-response relationships that track well with management zones.
- The crowding literature can help guide this research.

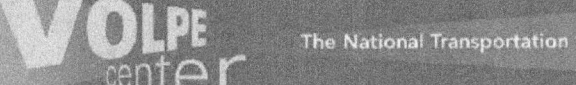

Initial lessons from the past

Future data: Be consistent with "core" of past studies:
- Core responses with same "scales"
- Core doses
- Core mediators, especially those found useful in past
—concentrating on those with "all-site coverage"

Potentially add responses, doses and mediators specific to new types of site.

For future data-taking, I hope we can be consistent with the "core" data of the past studies. Most important data types are the ones with complete past data.

The pending re-analysis

- First-cut regressions:
  - Selected responses, basic doses
  - Choose combinations to carry forward
- More-detailed regressions:
  - Select dose augmentations that improve the fit
- Regressions with mitigating variables:
  - Improve the fit further
  - Cross-validate by "site"

Results: Dose-response relations and their uncertainties

First-cut regressions would use just selected responses. More-detailed regressions select various dose augmentations. For example, % time audible could be augmented by the magnitude of the noise during those times (composite dose). Relative dose, tour level aircraft – the environmental/ambient noise. I will use methods that combine doses.

Comments:

- The goal should be not to find the best predictor, rather to determine whether there are any we can exclude.
- Are there predictors that emerge in an analysis that might be the result of random variation, statistically significantly different than the ones the agencies have available to use for management tools?
- Pay as much attention to the standard errors and confidence intervals as to the relationship itself.

- The focus should be on the regression coefficients to see if the dose-estimate is effective when measured against them.
- Indicators, standards, inventory, and monitoring. Somehow NPS has to be able to drop a monitoring device and determine what is occurring.
  - What is the dose management that is possible? What would we get from the more comprehensive and expensive measures of dose.
  - If you give them variables, the NPS manager thinks- where do we draw the line? Instead, what is the visitor feedback if there is a problem? Can they backwards relate to the negative letters, emails, comments, etc?

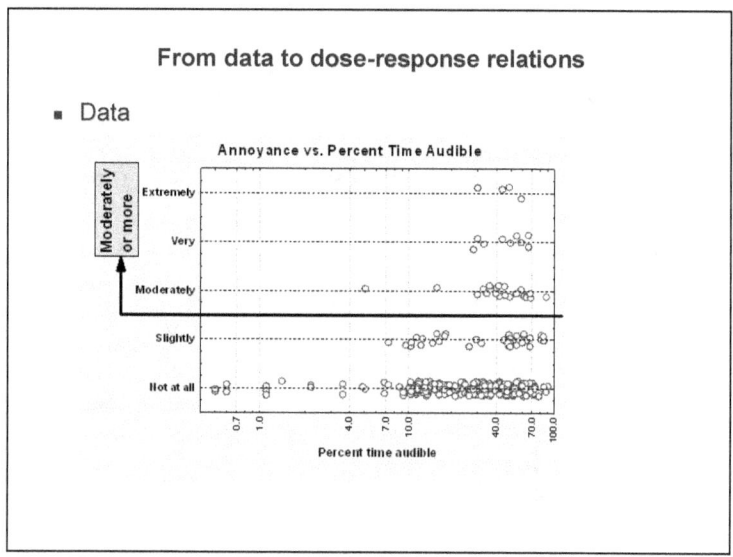

The 3rd step in the suggested analysis adds mitigating variables. Improve fit further and cross validate by site. We are attempting to obtain a percentage of time audible with % annoyance. In the graph, data have been "jittered" with Excel.

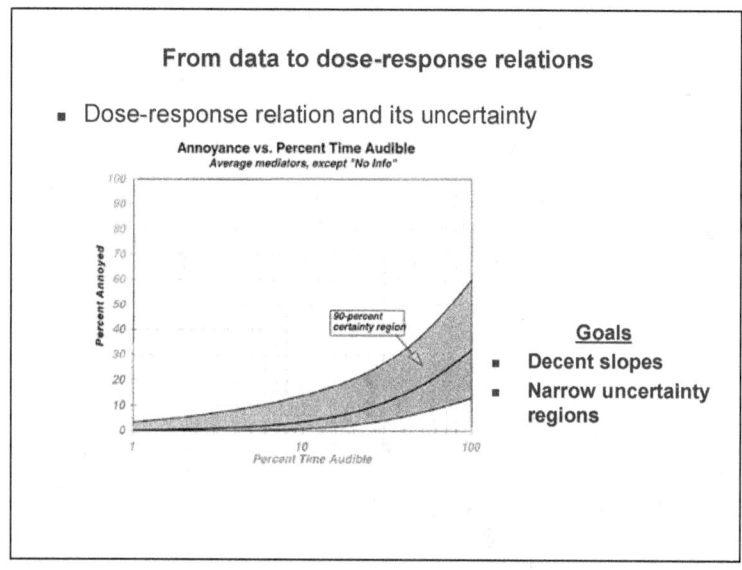

32

To narrow the uncertainty, use the type of site as one of your variables in the regression and that reduces some of the unexplained variability.

Comments:

- Duration of stay is also important.
- Most of the duration impacts have been examined.
- In the last study at some sites there were 2 distinct batches of visitors. When you looked at the groups they had differences. The 15-minute visitors had a very different impact than those who stayed for 1 hour.
- Motivation may be a stronger factor than length of stay. Motivation affects length of stay.

Decent slopes

- Slopes depend upon the dose metric and augmentations.

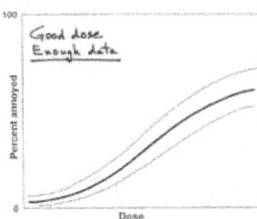
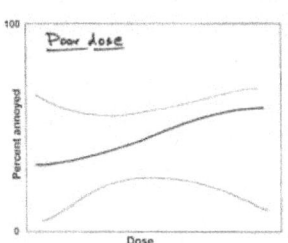

Future data: Continue to determine many dose metrics. Perhaps eliminate some, per pending re-analysis.

We combined the mediators in an interactive way. Slide as an example with a poor dose vs. a good dose. In the future, consider many dose metrics and perhaps eliminate some. The uncertainty region is generally good in areas that there are a lot of data, but diverges (uncertainty increases) for small and higher dose exposures. A good slope means there is a curve, rather than flat line, indicating a relationship.

Comments:

- If you don't have strong data at some sites it may negatively affect the predictive ability of the combination.

Narrow uncertainty regions

- Uncertainty less:
  - When dose relates "tightly" to the response.
  - With lots of data (both visitors and sites).

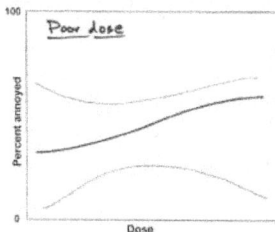
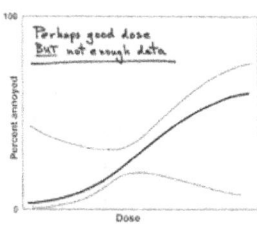

Future data: Measure lots of visitors, at lots of sites.

The next few slides discuss certainty/uncertainty of the data. All prior analyses only show uncertainty in the regression coefficients – Regression coefficients are long-term average. Part of this uncertainty is due to visitor variability and part is due to site variability. When dose-response is applied to only one site at a time, the uncertainty region grows dramatically.

Balance between sites and visitors

- Uncertainly less when have a good "balance" between # visitors and # sites.

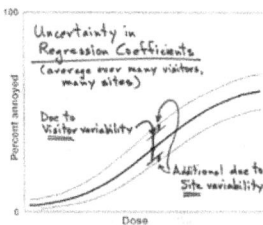

Future data: Learn visitor-site "balance" from pending re-analysis.

During application: <u>Site variability</u> most important

- Visitor variability averages out.
- Site variability does not, because only one site.

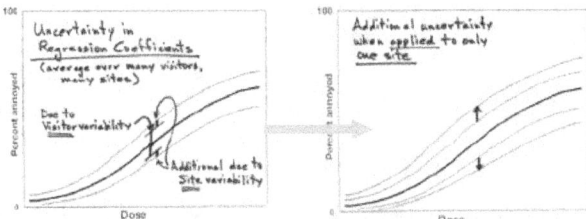

Future data: Minimize "unexplained" site variability
(variability not accounted for by regression variables).

Minimize "unexplained" site variability

- Well-chosen site mediators:
  - Site type
  - Percent helicopters
  - Others for existing site types?
  - Others for new site types (new contexts)?

- Must be:
  - Based in "science"
  - Not too many.

Minimize "unexplained" site variability

- Well-chosen site mediators:
  - Site type
  - Percent helicopters
  - Others for existing site types?
  - Others for new site types (new contexts)?

- Must be:
  - Based in "science"
  - Not too many.

So we need to minimize site uncertainty. Can choose well-selected site mediators (site type, percent helicopters, others for existing site types, new sites?)

- If the NPS managers have supplied data on15 characteristics that they are selecting for and we can only examine13 sites there is a problem.

Minimize "unexplained" site variability

- Well-chosen dose scales:

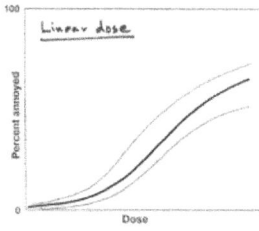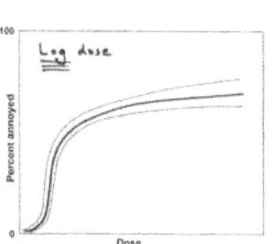

  - Dose scale determines regression shape.
  - Some shapes are a better fit than others.

This slide illustrates linear dose vs. logarithmic dose. Past studies should not determine identification of the optimal dose.

Comments:

- Look at the coefficients of different variables to see if the overlooks are picking up an over exposure.

This is an illustration of the idea of composite dose – can augment the dose with Leq aircraft vs. background Leq.

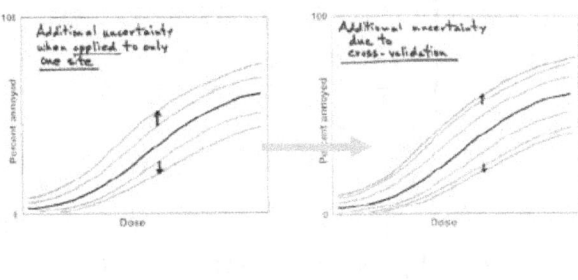

Cross validation increases the predictive uncertainty further. You know the variables in the regression. You then leave out a site and re-regress, then compare that new regression to the data for the site that was removed. Weighting can occur by number of respondents. Then repeat with each of the other sites left out, one at a time.

Comments:

- That is the standard method for calculation of standard errors and confidence intervals.
- That is what we did during prior analyses (term: jack-knifing).

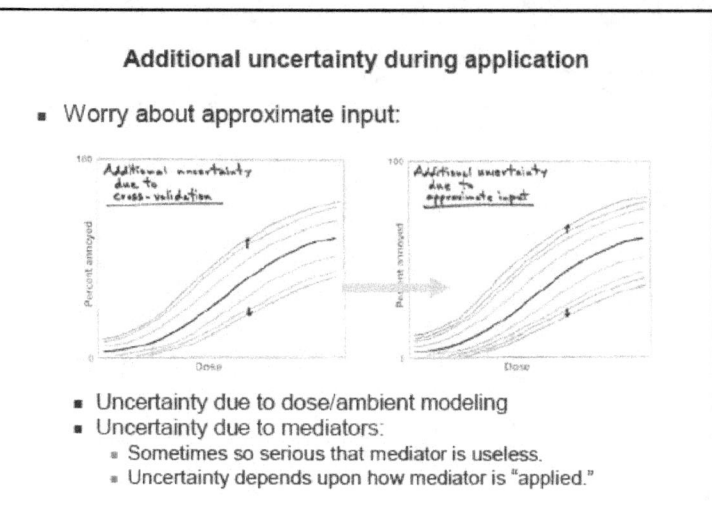

Additional uncertainty during application

- Worry about approximate input:
    - Uncertainty due to dose/ambient modeling
    - Uncertainty due to mediators:
        - Sometimes so serious that mediator is useless.
        - Uncertainty depends upon how mediator is "applied."

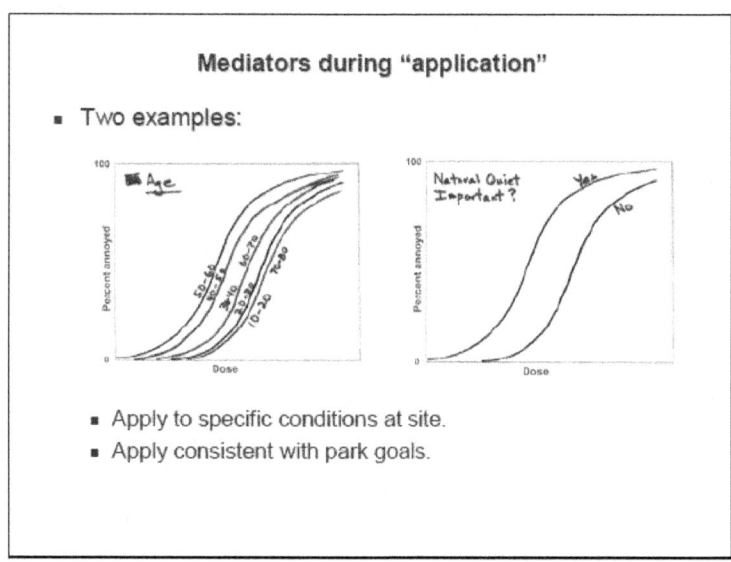

Mediators during "application"

- Two examples:
    - Apply to specific conditions at site.
    - Apply consistent with park goals.

Input uncertainty. For %Time Audible, most likely NPS will use the INM, which predicts percent time audible for the site (not the individual). So we won't have individual doses. Also, we will have approximate values of other input.

Comments:

- To get some realism, get some NPS managers estimations of age and then see if their imprecise estimates of data will reduce the uncertainty. For the purpose of the management tool the question is whether this approximation for age reduces the amount of the uncertainty.
- If people were not expecting natural quiet on their visit, perhaps they are less annoyed when they hear the aircraft sound. At Mount Rushmore, if visitors are not there to experience natural quiet, you could substitute a "no" curve and increase the accuracy of the prediction.
- When the parks go to make a management zone you can take parts and pieces that will equate with certain curves.

- We are no longer predicting the % of people that will be affected. We are instead identifying the response of those in a particular sensitive subgroup and are not concerned about the relative number of people in different subgroups.
- There are a wide range of parks and people could self-select to find another park, or location as an alternative.

Summary: Main lessons

- Retain "core" responses, doses, mediators
  —especially those with complete past coverage.
- New site types:
  - Measure lots of visitors, at lots of sites.
  - Learn visitor/site "balance" from pending re-analysis.
  - Determine many dose metrics/augmentations.
  - Perhaps add new variables (responses, doses, mediators).
- Doses and mediators:
  - Work hard to minimize "unexplained" site variability.
  - Worry about uncertainty during application.
  - "Apply" consistent with park goals.

In Summary, we should retain the core responses, measure data at new site types.

Comments:

- One benefit to correcting for site variability you can use fewer sites. Haven't done the analysis from the past studies. We will we learn the balance between the number of visitors and sites subject to funding constraints.
- After mapping management zones – you will have then have management standards. For example, the number of visitors for crowding - the same could be applied to sound levels.
- Aircraft noise spreads over an enormous area, so impacts to a backcountry user will reduce the need to manage for front country (overlooks/short hike) if the management is only for the most sensitive group. Sound might not be able to be assessed independently.
- People also flow over the woods over a time sequence. There is a masking effect were people will not hear aircraft until they are in a more remote location.

-Break-

Agenda Item: Discuss Research Framework and Characterize Proto-type Dose-Response Sites

Purpose: Discuss steps that will lead to informed research on how visitors to national parks are likely to respond to aircraft noise, (Table 1). Identify proto-type sites for discussion of dose-response data acquisition. Review/revise factors with which to characterize sites, and develop proto-type sites based on alternative combinations of site factors (Table 2, the final edited version of these Tables are in Appendix B)

- These Tables outline simple ways to determine the next steps, because on Day 3 we want to create an actual timeline to determine how much time this will require.

Discussion: Characterize/Prioritize Sites

Table 2 provides a relative gauge on how important is it to obtain information – so we can provide opinions on what types are important. The framework is focused primarily on data acquisition efficiency. To get the process going, NPS and researchers have opinions of where we would like to gather data. There are ~90 parks to gather data and perhaps on average 4-5 sites per park. We need to do some exclusion.

- We can perhaps do some exclusion due to the characteristics of the park. For example, the gain some exclusion we could potentially avoid the Grand Canyon based on the press of high levels of visitation.
- A major effect may be to get people to move away from noisy sites or parks and thus to reduce the number of people visiting parks. This is called "Displacement". What are the main variables we need to study? If there are a number of site variables, we need a wide distribution of sites. NPS is likely to have to manage "zones" across the parks.
  - There could multiple park management plans on a single park (e.g., Wild and Scenic Rivers in Yosemite). Merced and Touloumne have 2 different management plans.
- [Referring to Table 2] Site vs. Area – what kind of "site" is it? Confined, linear (trail) distributed broad area (valley)? We want the NPS to express priorities by management concerns.
  - Have them identify areas of management interest in respect to air tours. NPS might provide a list of areas and each area may have a list of descriptors and then the researchers should make choices of what fits into research needs.
  - Would there be sites that would be excluded if NPS selects only some sites?
  - Places of high visitor use where people could potentially be affected by air tours.
  - Outstanding recreational value areas (ORV) might be a place with a high priority location.
- We are at the first level of developing a sampling process. What is the most effective list of sites for a broad level of sampling?
  - NPS selects general types of areas and we select sites that are primarily based on cost.
  - The problem is filling in holes in our knowledge. We need to fill in the areas where we don't have data. What are the types of sites that represent the variables they think are most important? Then we can start to figure out cost features.
- Create a range front country to remote recreation area. VERP actually identifies sites and can be used to categorize areas with a site.
- What are the types of sites that affect people, and will affect an individual's response? How are we going to parameterize these?
- What determines our ability to collect data? It is up to NPS to determine the important visitor aspects to measure.
- If NPS provides a list of sites they would like to study, it will exceed research time/money available. We can select from the list and create priorities. We would expect NPS to express a range of sites that represent a major set of activities.
  - What are the types of zones that you manage differently?
  - As an example: There are 127 sites and 39 "noise sensitive" sites at Grand Canyon that NPS has identified as priority sites with noise - they span a range of contexts. NPS usually wants information for far more sites

The National Transportation Systems Center   U.S. Department of Transportation
Research and Innovative Technology Administration

than we can measure. Sites selected from various stakeholder input and through the process of multiple NEPA analyses additional sites were selected.

- o Some subjective features are going in to NPS judgment on site identification. What do we want to ask a whole batch of managers? Not sure that the Grand Canyon would be the ideal model of site selection.
- We need NPS input for what types of variables we should study or where we should be going. We need the information to efficiently design studies.
- Using Table 2 if we select the range, we can talk about the methods. When we get a list shouldn't we be able to state that "this would be difficult to accomplish", and the related reasons.
- Is there a list of locations that don't have air tour plans that need them?
  - o One third have more than 5000 tours, 1/3 5000-1000 tours, 1/3 less than 1000 tours. They are prioritized mostly by sites with the most air tours.
  - o It is not just air tour noise in parks that we are interested in; FAA is interested in all of it. Air tours are a focus, but they recognize that all aircraft overflights are of interest.
  - o There is no getting away with avoiding the cumulative effects of aircraft noise.
  - o The criteria we have for prioritizing the sites then aligns with FAA goals.
  - o NPS likes the audibility metric – FAA needs to know when the aircraft are audible, even at 30,000 feet.
- Within this group we have some sort of understanding of what the challenges are and what would make it more difficult to gather. We need to have some sort idea on how to address the challenges, for example, to address backcountry measurement difficulties. We may have differences on how to do it, but collectively our discussions can inform a questionnaire for the parks. We are not doing an "entire" world of sounds or doing wildlife. We are concerned about certain variables, NPS has a very extensive list of concerns, let's find the world of sites.

Take-away: New item on Table 1: Develop an NPS site survey, with a list of contexts relevant to dose-response.

Discussion: Optimize Sampling Plan (# of sites / # of visitors per site)

- Is there any need to get statistically sound data collection estimations to determine the optimal number of sites?
  - o Plug in the unit cost per site and compare it to the statistical requirements to determine a minimum number of sites.
- We need to know a number of site characteristics to determine data collection needs. From NPS data - # visitors, areas (sq feet) of coverage, # of air tours, etc.
- We could use the existing data to determine the balance between number of future sites vs the number of visitors surveyed at each site—or we can do a pretest to get early data and apply those results.
- At some point we are going to need to have estimates of site variability and we will need to know what conditions we will study and then we will need sites to satisfy each of these requirements. At that point, we can exercise the statistical models that include site variability to combine with the conditions to determine how many cells in a design and sites we need.
- Make decisions based on an iterative process that includes the existing sites and each incremental addition.
- Is there an advantage to conducting backcountry visits in locations where we have already covered front country sites?
  - o Everything, ideally, should be framed as site specific, rather than park specific. If we try to understand park-to-park differences, we are opening up a Pandora's box that would require substantial additional research (many, many parks).
- If we are only talking about 5 sites and NPS has to limit their choices are we making it difficult for them to decide?
  - o We may want to first submit an open question to NPS and then make a decision. At White Sands, we wanted to measure the effects of military operations on visitors. We then moved into logistics which

 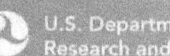
created a process to cull the list. The reductive process wasn't that bad. We can create the worst case scenario in this room.

Take-aways: New Items on Table 1:

o Perform statistical analyses using current data to make decisions about the number of new sites needed
o Distill and present results to NPS / FAA; it is the beginning of a process that should have been started initially – why has this not been used/what are we missing?

Discussion: Site – Prototypes (Table 2). How are we going to evaluate sites from a research feasibility standpoint?

If we come up with 4-5 proto-typical sites that haven't been investigated we may be able to think about how we going to proceed. (Referring to Table 2) Are they linear-hike or dispersed-area? How many visitor points of entry / how do you get the visitors (are there some natural places to capture them)?

• Make some summary judgment with the difficulty of data acquisition
• How about "Shielded portions"? Are there buildings that will affect visitor exposures and experience? Add new column [Table 2] for the shielded portion? Have to determine when they enter and exit. Thinking about sound attenuation indoors (windows open, closed, etc.)
• On a prototype basis we can think about a battlefield. Considering a "drive-up" experience. Site with historical significance and thinking about potential sacred nature of a site.
• Second – Daylong (or extended) day hike (one trail) - visitation would be moderate, trails often have limited access points, there are special considerations such as water sources.
• Third Backcountry Destination
  o One major issue is adequate sample size - a major trail junction supports measurement efforts.
  o Ideally we are looking for a one-day experience, e.g., a 4-hour hike to a destination, time at a destination, and then returning to the start.
  o There are different sensitivities along the way and on the journey vs. the destination.
  o How can you determine the distinction between the journey and the destination?
• We can add [to the list of proto-type sites] interpretive talks, bird watching, sacred nature of site/appreciation.
• The fourth site-type is multi-Day Backcountry
• One way to look at it might be to look at the NPS designation of sites (National Scenic Rivers, National Recreation sites, National Historic Parks, Parks with more of a cultural approach).
  o We have been looking at zones within parks as the unit of analysis since the park units themselves can have multiple zones within a single park.
• On Table 1, there is a universe of types of places within parks, and if we can get a list of places what would that universe be? What we want to know is what is out there. Maybe we would obtain a listing with a few variables that they can check off - then narrow the list (refinement), once we match these with the measurement variables. We need to get down to a handful of places to test hypothesis or add to the value of dose-response.
• If you look at GMP (general management plans) of different parks you could correlate the zones to NPS management zones – this could line up with the indicators and the resulting standards.
  o At some point we need to assess what we are doing and how it can be generalized to the management zones that get laid upon the landscape.
  o The framework of picking these is very important. Major national parks have a huge number of management schemes within national parks.
  o We may want to look at VERP and use those definitions.

 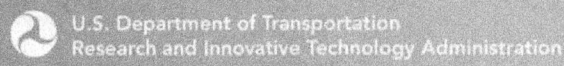
- Do we need to go one more step beyond and give us something beyond extended day hike? If we believe that duration will have significant influence on dose, do we need something that is in between a short hike and an extended day hike?
- Does seasonal variation have a worthwhile difference?
- Developed (built environment) vs. front country?
- Different sites will have different ranges of exposure. If you have limited variability at a site that will affect the data gathering. (You will need more sites)
- The longer the exposure, the more the variation in dose between individuals will decrease.
- One of the first things to list on the challenges of backcountry measurement is weather.

Take-away: Proto-type sites are initially classified as : Multi-day backcountry, Day-hike backcountry, Frontcountry-Short Hike, Frontcountry Overlook, Frontcountry Developed, Interpretive Talk, Battlefield (dispersed historic), Historic (Concentrated), Historic (Indoor?) (See completed Table 2)

-Break-

Agenda Item: Design data acquisition methods for proto-type sites

Purpose: Identify challenges and propose solutions for data acquisition at each proto-type site, **Table 3**

- Dispersed areas are particularly challenging.
- Lots of people and many different doses is what we are after. At Hawaii Volcanoes variability in dose came with hiking concentration.
- Trails helped define the noise corridors in Hawaii Volcanoes; airplanes and people travelled in parallel which made it easier.
- One of the challenges is that air tours don't want to discuss where they fly.
- The noise map would need to be dynamic across time for a dispersion model.
  - At Rocky Mountain we are doing the noise surface transportation with a static model and GPS trackers to assess location overlay on the noise map. Visitors carry the unit, and the transponders give location at 5 second intervals which we correlate with a noise map.

Discussion: Noise Dose Estimation Methods in Dispersed Areas

Re: Modeling

- If air traffic is irregular and dispersed it may be difficult accurately estimate (map) dose.
- Modeling is problematic for air tours. Visitors don't distinguish between air tours and General Aviation, so we need to track both.
- We can get aircraft location information with photo triangulation. You can get slant measurements if you know the focal distance of the lens and the approach angle. Using three photo sites and a sound meter could yield source data.
  - This method could be expensive to process even if the data gathering is less expensive.
  - This could cover an area the size of acres. If the visitors are dispersed over the landscape it is difficult.
- We can determine the loudness of the aircraft. The aircraft are basically cruising so sound level doesn't vary much. Some seasonal employee can keep track of the aircraft over the course of a summer and the only piece of data is missing is route information.
  - Don't rule out air tour cooperation at this point. It may not be a completely lost cause.

- o   Parks with Air Tour Management plans have known air tour routes.
- We have more aircraft we can have more averaging. We need to be careful about how we model estimates for doses because there could be statistical errors in such estimates.

Re: Visitor-Based Sound Level Monitors (Dosimeters)

- I used a sound recorder to measure my backpacking sounds and then merged sounds of aircraft obtained from the web. I pulled out ½ second A-level Leqs. 1/10 second durations would have been preferable, but more expensive.
  - o   It could be pilot tested with a few backpackers and some dosimeters.
  - o   Need to conduct extensive noise monitoring at the same time.
  - o   It could be tested by researchers at a local GA airport with low traffic, or a location that is easy to conduct and provide it to visitors.
- If there is a wire associated, we may have a low rate of success. Weight may be a factor (1/2 pound).
- Worry about putting the sensor on a backpack, with people putting it down and leaving it while they have lunch and damaging the unit by putting it down with force.
- You might have difficulty determining aircraft from noise ratio so data gathered may be limited in nature.- Can't adjust for a car, stream, etc.
- These monitors don't capture content, just sound level and frequency?
  - o   There are audio recorders that are light and can be implanted on a hat and capture type of noise, unfortunately they also capture conversation.
  - o   There is a European cell phone based recorded noise program that we could learn from. Enrollment and contribution of data is elective.

Take-away: Test of 3 methods: For Dispersed-Area Measurements, we would need to test dose estimation methods: Direct Measure, Model, and Dosimeter.

Day 2

Goals for the day: Continue discussion and edit tables 2 and 3.

Take-aways from day 1:

- Set up detailed tests to simultaneously compare methods for measuring or estimating dose over wide-areas (add to Table 4).
  - o Dosimeter
    - Assess the human behavior impact on the accuracy of the dosimeter estimation.
    - Can get a good test regardless of location.
    - If in-site, do we need a researcher to pair up with each visitor?
  - o Modeling.
    - Major hurdle is how to get detailed information on flight patterns / tracks?
      - Photography slant distance with known flight-tracks.
      - Radar? (for flight tracking) It is incredibly expensive and it might be about $100K for one month's rental.
- Example: Pick an area like White Sands, measure as in previous tests, measure by handing out dosimeters to visitors, also model using photographs of aircraft to determine slant distance from visitor. Ideally the flight tracks would be parallel to visitors travel
- What is the "gold standard" method?

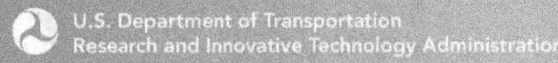

VOLPE center   The National Transportation Systems Center   U.S. Department of Transportation Research and Innovative Technology Administration

- Terrain may dictate the method of choice.

Discussion: Issues associated with battlefield site prototype.(con't)

- Issue: historic sites probably require new survey questions.
- Issue: Tracking visitors at sites where there may be an infinite number of visit entrances/exits or corridors. There also may be multiple destinations and activities.
  - ○ Possibly concentrate on a handful of locations within a site.
  - ○ The multiple entry/exit problem has been addressed in biological studies - the park service has kept up with those.
- Take-away: We need to inventory certain site types such as battlefields and assess how they differ. And we need to assess how that type of site can be generalized.

Discussion: Site Scoping

- An on-site scoping visit should always be conducted first to assess how people interact with a location. With a single day of scoping you can generally get a sense of visitor behavior.
- NPS has detailed information on visitation such as time at certain sites and visitor movement in parking lots etc. Data gathering varies from park to park.
- Different parks may require different amounts of scoping. Grand Canyon backcountry assessment may take more than a couple of days.

Different activities (like bird watching) may require changes to the surveys and timing of the data collection. We may need some specific questions for certain activities and certain testing and accommodations for data gathering for those activities.

Discussion: Interpretive talks

- For interpretive talks we have no data (add to Table 2). We have telephone interviews with 20 rangers from parks that have reported that there potential issues. Whenever there were two or more "events" during a talk we hear complaints from rangers and/or visitors.
- Although this category of site-prototype may not be the most sensitive overall, it is useful to obtain data for management goals - there are locations where this may be the most sensitive use.
- Interpretative talks might be one of the rare instances when we can directly observe and record the dose.
  - ○ Easy to send data gatherer(s) who can monitor the group (record behavioral responses) and record the noise exposure (audibility).
  - ○ Most interpretative talks are short (1/2 hour or less)
- Issue: The signal to noise ratio may vary at a talk for the audience members that are farther from the ranger/speaker.
  - ○ We need to know the speaker's voice level for interpretative talks.
  - ○ If we deal with this level of detail there are measurement challenges with distance speaker-audience distance, speaker volume, etc.
  - ○ We just need noise measurement in one location for the group talk.
- Issue: The survey would be different because we need to assess if the content of the talk is affected by the aircraft noise.
  - ○ Big picture questions are 1) Are visitors getting experience that NPS expects and 2) are the visitors getting the information from talks.
- Issue: Are different dose metrics needed?

 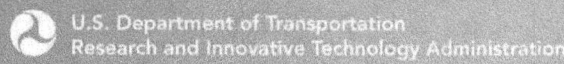
- Take-away: Interpretive talks should be listed as a priority site due their status as a 'known' issue and the relative ease of data collection.

Discussion: Survey Intercept Timing for Longer-duration Visits (>4 hours)

- Question: Is it important or necessary to measure response 'as it happens', or can the survey intercept occur at the end of the hike (or the end of the visit)?   Is it meaningful to get the measure on an average? Do we want the response after a single event or after the entire experience
- Useful for park managers to know both pieces of information – when they hear the noise and what they think at the end of the hike.
    - We could assess the superintendents with the question: how does the park service feel about experiences that are out of character with the park experience even if those experiences might not be recalled on completion of the activity.   The tolerance that people experience with noise varies over time and we may find that over time we integrate the experience in a way that noise does not result in an impact.

- Known issues:
    - There is recall error. Memories will be revised over time.
        - Cognitive research show memory goes from discrete to synthesis over time. Synthesis is almost always "happy."
        - There is some time threshold where this becomes a problem, as you could go from one mode of processing to another from a biological standpoint.
        - If there is an impact and no one remembers it, has there been an impact? NPS would probably argue that there has been an impact.
        - With solitude, "encounters" are measured on an hourly basis, otherwise they get diluted.
        -
    - Noise becomes noticed with multiple exposures. Multiple exposures will increase annoyance. Ideally we will know how many events it takes to generate annoyance. The annoyance will be generated by a wide range of memories.

- Take-away: We should study response as function of duration within visit. Study the effects on response between events shortly after they occur vs. the integration of a collective experience.
    - Sometimes we are limited by the problem by the logistics of backcountry so we have to generalize the experience. Because of those challenges we typically administer the survey at the conclusion (exit trailhead) of their experience.
    - If you took a series of points you could measure the time intervals to obtain a better understanding of the relationship between time of dose and time of measurement. 1 hour intervals? Half hour intervals?
    - There would be problems with sample size: as soon as we ask a question, we cannot ask that visitor the same question again, later on.

Discussion: How will the results of this research inform management?

- The research should help to cooperatively manage the airspace over parks using scientific tools.
    - The prior LEQ studies will be used now in a way that noise studies haven't been used in the past 10-15 years. One big contribution from the visitor dose-response might demonstrate that NPS doesn't have to worry that each site demands a tailored study to determine dose-response.
- Is there an option to get connected with the NPS stakeholders?
    - Twice a year there is a national group that meets on wilderness issues and there could be an educational component (primer) so that participants can get up to speed on noise.

The National Transportation Systems Center · U.S. Department of Transportation Research and Innovative Technology Administration

- We are conducting research because it may change the way the FAA conducts business. We will have to share the information with FAA stakeholders. We recognize that we are very far behind on wilderness issues and the more interagency dialogue we can engage in the better.

-Break-

Discussion: How to get variation in dose for multi-day visits

Issue: The longer duration that is included in the dose, the less difference there will be between the doses experienced by different visitors. There is probably no variation in exposure in any one site for multi-day visitation.

- Would there be variation between weekdays and weekends?
- Flights are not greatly different between the days. We could potentially "turn on" and "turn off" aircraft to achieve a control.
  - We ought to be able to have air tour operators fly certain routes and elevations so we can get a better control of exposure so that we can accurately estimate that exposure. Dialogue between tour operators and FAA/NPS would be necessary.
  - NPOAG members may agree to participate.
  - This ability is critical and the cost of the research may be reduced with this coordination.
- Take-away: Explore the possibility of controlled flights with tour operators/NPAOG.

Discussion – How will results be incorporated into ATMPs

Question to FAA/NPS - What is the one thing you need from the research?

- We should have 2-3 ATMP documents a year minimum for the next several years with a goal to get 30-40 completed.
  - If the most important ATMP are conducted now this research will only influence the less important parks?
  - Is anyone going to be able to alter these ATMP documents once the dose-response is ready? This is analogous to changing the 65 DNL standard.
  - If the reanalysis of the data is conducted and there are more solid results from the study, the FAA will want to use that research. We need something (in the area of visitor impact) and we don't have anything.
  - It would be better if the first draft of the Grand Canyon would have dose-response work included. If this is introduced at a later date we will likely have a great deal of push back from air tour operators and have to justify it extensively.
- The sooner the result comes out the better. What compelling result can be conducted even if only affects a moderate amount of situations. Getting to "a" good result is more important that tackling the largest problem.
- It would be helpful to get together the top "three" gaps to prioritize the work. FAA doesn't have any criteria, to inform the decision making.
- NPS would use data, and even without backcountry user we can still use the findings for the upper bound of annoyance.

Discussion: Sound Source identification

- Aircraft is just one source. We should distinguish between, and get information about, other sources of sound.
- There were some issues brought about by the previous hierarchal methods of sound-source logging. But, we now have a handheld unit where we can distinguish between sources.

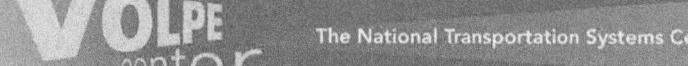

- How would we get aircraft audibility without field observers?
  - The method NPS uses differentiate when a sound level is "on" or "off" via continual audio and 1/8 octave sensing via a machine.
  - However, the issues of non-aircraft anthropogenic sources and masking have not been addressed.
- Takeaway: Continue studies of live source-identification vs. machine. Automated source-identification could be used anywhere and over long periods of time.

Site Ambient

There are places where we could learn what the local environment is. The narrow concern is that this is a significant mediator? A potential factor is what the general noise has on a response to aircraft noise.

- Will the manager know that removal of a sound source will make the aircraft sound stand out more?
- Park managers can alter transportation habits to affect the ambient at the site.
- Natural ambient can be subtracted from the aircraft noise.
- If ambient is a dose-response indicator from past studies, it would be good to obtain visitor specific local ambient as a mediating factor.

Indoor Impacts

Are we going to determine sound levels (and dose-response) for indoor spaces, etc?

- In eastern US, most of the sites are historical buildings – it would be useful to get NPS focus group opinion on this issue.
- If protecting outdoor space one can assume that the less sensitive environment is indoors.
  - San Antonio Mission may be an exception as it is managed for a reverential environment.
- Most visitors spend a significant amount of time in developed sites. That may affect the way they are experiencing the natural environment.
- This changes the whole nature of how we are thinking about the research. This may introduce a level of complexity may slow the process a great deal.
- We have excluded sites that have any structure that the participants can go into.
- This is probably not the first criteria that we would be concerned over.
- All aircraft noise should be considered as airports and General Aviation will have impact.
- Take-away: Indoor sites will most-likely be less sensitive. This research would be lower on the priority list.

Key Point: We need to direct our focus at the sensitive sites and hours. For example, we are so far excluding 80% of hours when there is less visitation (evenings, Fall trough Spring months, etc).

Campgrounds:

Campground study is needed.

- Front country campground research is valuable.
- Is it necessary to determine information for a back country camp setting, as the assumption is that the visitor is protected via the other dose-response work?
  - The backcountry camper may have different sensitivities than the hiker.
  - Understanding while hiking vs. reflective at the campground it may be useful.
  - There is an indicator for crowding for hiking and a separate one of campgrounds.
- Do we need to look at dose response in day and night as NPS manages differently for day and evening standards? Obtaining empirical data would help us make those decisions.

- o   Background ambient typically drops during evening.
- Following one logic, however, it is whichever one is most sensitive that is important because that is the one to manage and that is thus the type of condition that we need empirical data to support?
- From a management perspective the protection of the acoustical environment in the remote backcountry would likely be sufficient to protect these other environments.
- If the focus is on high sensitivity then key research may center on the timing of aircraft during sensitive midday activities, and shoulders (sunrise/sunset)
- Take-aways: a) Campgrounds (both front-country and back-country) should likely be listed as a prototype site; and b) Focus research on most sensitive sites.

-Break-Lunch

Discussion: Bob Manning joined by teleconference.

Dr. Manning was briefed on the discussions thus far, and offered the following comments:

- Park superintendents might not be the best to assess the work. Some of the resource managers might be useful at specific parks. The planning staff at the Denver service center might be more qualified to comment on the research.
- At Muir Woods visitors are allowed to experience the park and then we conduct "simulations."
- With crowding, conflicting uses, environmental impacts in questionnaires we describe a range of variables that are acceptable or appropriate (e.g. if you saw a person every 10 minutes would that be acceptable). Where appropriate we also use visual simulations. What is so bad that people would be driven away from a park? We have taken this approach for Muir Woods to provide scenarios for the park.
- The clips were designed so that we know the acoustic characteristics of the clips. The first set of clips were aesthetically constructed so we knew the sound at the ear, the next were parametrically selected using the 1/3 octave band. Stepped up in 2 dB sound levels.
- Can we design the dose-response curve in the field, highly controlled by the researcher, with a neutral point on the range and such research can support a standard of quality. We might be able to generalize beyond individual sites in individual parks.
- It might extend beyond sound clip, narrative and numerical questions may be a place to begin. It may be reasonable to inquire about the acceptability of the frequency of aircraft sound.
- Take away: Compare results of audio clips compared to the "brand name" (standard) dose-response approach.

Agenda Item: Variables to Measure Universally

Purpose: Discuss Response, Mediator and Dose variables to collect across studies, Tables 5a, 5b, 5c

Discussion: Table 5A – Response variables

In developing this table, I have thought about the noise variables, and comments that we can't manage annoyance because it is a negative concept while the NPS goal is to promote a positive goal of enjoyment or particular experiences. Dealing with questions that would be good to develop a model about what situations and what people are bothered. NPS wants to manage to the positive experiences that people should have at a site. This is the quality of experiences that people have at the site regarding specific dimensions (values in chart) that fit into NPS management goals. So the ultimate goal may be to predict whether or not visitors had a "top quality" experience of natural quiet. A question is whether the natural quiet enjoyment measure may be biased by cognitive dissonance (i.e. all the money, time, and effort expended to visit a site may create an incentive to believe an experience is enjoyable). If one can get past this tendency, it may be possible to measure perceived quality of particular experiences.

- If an individual is asked about their experience at the Grand Canyon, they might state enjoyment or achieving solitude and if I then ask about seeing aircraft then people might want to go back to the enjoyment question.
- Importance/Performance allows comparison of the variables, but in practice we have found the results "boring" it may be because variables are linked to cognitive dissonance. These are generally ranked on a 1-5 rating and the results are generally that everything is "peachy." The values of these variables don't have enough variation between them.
  - Are there alternative scales or question wordings that will help? You have to do something that is less broad to get better results.
- Management wants to know if aircraft come in are we degrading the quality of the experience for visitors. Every time we bring up more specifics we can bring out attitudes towards a source.
- Study the variables to evaluate the measures of visitor experience.
- Are there measures that you can get without interjecting a standard? Using acceptability or appropriateness adds a judgment dimension to the study. The NPS has a role is to decide what experiences should happen at certain sites. From the research, however, they would want to know, for example, the extent to which visitors experienced solitude. We want to find out about the quality of the experience. Also interested in what they were looking for and if it was up to what the park service provides.
- It is helpful to understand what they think is appropriate and what they derive from an experience.
- Add appropriateness and "extent that you have experienced (x)? to the table?
- Make a global list and include things like preference and displacement.
- We are going through all of this to add 2-3 questions to the survey? What is our goal?
- We don't have questions with positive scales that could be useful to park managers. We also get a few key measures we did not have before.
  - At White Sands we conducted a probe of visitors and found that they did understand "natural quiet."
- Significant terms that apply in legislation, such as "solitude", we are bound to address them even if they are difficult to evaluate empirically.
- What are the choices we have to make using a finite range of questions? That will help develop model and management tool. It is expensive to develop the sites, so it would be great if we could get a baseline from other conducted studies.

Retain Questions from Original Studies

Some of the assumptions on what we are doing here, we want to retain the core questions from the original questionnaires.

- We can't afford to lose the original studies. Anything we do, I assume that we will have questions that will either duplicate the questions from the previous studies or will be very close in wording and have been proved to provide dose-response relations that are identical to previous studies.
- We are maintaining the "series" going forward. We can actually present the old questionnaire and the new one at the same time to different visitors within the same visitor group for the purposes of calibration.
- Is it also an assumption that we are trying to relate all the studies to each other. What are we carrying forward?
  - (1) Were you bothered or annoyed by aircraft noise during your visit to this site (5-point scale)? and (2) How much did sound from aircraft interfere with your appreciation of the natural quiet and sounds of nature at this site? These are the two essential questions that should be carried into future dose-response data collection.
- If you have to fight with OMB, you might have a stronger case if you can argue that it is part of broad framework.

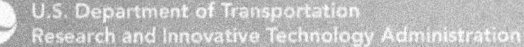
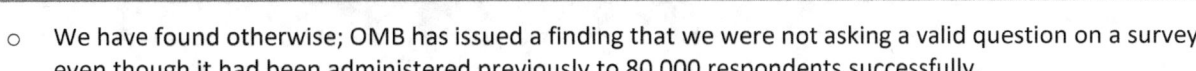

- o We have found otherwise; OMB has issued a finding that we were not asking a valid question on a survey even though it had been administered previously to 80,000 respondents successfully.
- If you want to ask questions at a site and 10 years later want to survey that site again, how you do that assessment again. How do we standardize the results?
  - o That is not clear. Instead of a longitudinal study might want to go to new sites with sites that we think have identical characteristics. The advantage then is that we could obtain several sites that were representative of the same types of soundscapes. We want to share questions from the start.
  - o The goal is to establish as much correspondence between studies and that might mean utilizing exact words.
  - o We want words that will fit into park service management objectives.
- Need environmental psychologists to get involved in question development (Paul and Britt). Emotions play a big role in our decisions. Cognitive dissonance
- Take away: Begin research on values (other than in the core questions) by assessing existing literature for existing "values" to know how people experience those values when exposed to aircraft sounds.

NOTE: Items on table 1 can run in parallel.

You should be able to take out the decision makers so they can experience the attended listening and understand the context.

- Before they make the decisions. As people go up the management scale they spend less and less time on the immediacy of noise as an issue.

Break

Discussion: Table 5B - Mediator Values

This list may be important. We have not measured the relative magnitude of their "importance." We have never asked "why are you visiting here."

- Should add motivation as an "attentiveness" mediator
- Group, gender, children sometimes made a difference, often contrary to expectations.
- First visit to park as is factor.
- Asking how long they have been in the park is important because the visitor may have become aware of the components (such as natural quiet) of the park and secondly expectation and the extent which people can form a set of expectations before they get to the park.
- Often the appreciation for the soundscape or natural quiet is a momentary concern. The question is it important for any moment of time to be able to access the natural quiet.
- Asking how many aircraft they heard gives us a sense of if they have been aware.
- The literature about visitor crowding and conflict may be relevant for understanding the effects of noise. Questionnaires should be short and it is terribly expensively to get some of the data if other variables have to be left off the survey.
- In the future we could eliminate some of these variables so that we can get some additional park management variables. One other source of information may be from the other visitor surveys (such as the non dose/response surveys from the early 1990s) and it may be useful to review if they would be useful.
- We should cross out the mediators that weren't significant from our first analyses. We may want to test if a mediator is important, once again, for some other mediators. We may want to include some for backcountry settings or to test once again that a mediator is not important for these new site types.
- If resource managers were asked for a list of potential mediators they would generate a large list. Maybe we would limit those variables for which they could manage.
- There is a whole set of mediators that are part of the dense body of research that have been conducted on crowding.

 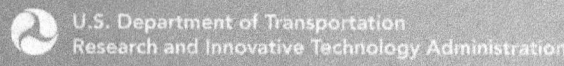

- Bob Manning has a great chapter in his book that has a summary of these mediators. We have thought about sounds in a similar way, and evaluation of sound can be deemed "noise." We have discussed how people have rendered judgments concerning density and ones that concern sounds
- Would it be effective to have a short lecture on crowding so that we can get the language and the concepts? We could also do a half hour session on noise metrics.
- After the reanalysis of the data, you will be able to tell which ones you can throw out?
  - o It may be a happy outcome if none the mediators affect the dose-response. At some point down the road we present the short list to the park service groups and determine if they have anything else.
- There is another crowding model from Bell et al. as applied to noise and includes the psychological effect of "coping." Coping covers many of the mediating variables.
- Signage is a factor like the research at White Sands. Signage did likely cause the visitors to adjust expectations accordingly.
  - o Signage in Denali in 2000 appears to have sensitized visitors and those who were pre-informed were more annoyed. However, acoustic data may not have been measured to assess dose so there might have been confounding factors.
  - o Take aways: Research mediators used in crowding literature. Eliminate variables from previous surveys which were not significant.

Tracking Visitors – Measuring Crowding

The crowdedness of a site is a potential mediator which has not been investigated previously.

- The Volpe team did not count the number of people who were skipped during interviewing.
- Presence can be tracked by observation, infra-red, and permits. We track use density by time. The precision that you measure that is different according to cost and site. We are tracking the number of bodies in a given area.
  - o Can you establish the group composition vs. absolute number of people?
  - o Can you get temporal or spatial headways? Is there any validity if the headway is small?
  - o Visitors that visit at different times may be part of temporal displacements.
  - o Can you separate those individuals who arrived early on?
- I would want to measure use-density and ask people's perception of crowding
- Take-away: For future studies, ask one objective and one subjective measure of crowding.

Acoustic Summaries

FAA would like inputs on other things that should be measured in order to compute people's exposure to noise. Are there other ones that NPS would like to include for acoustics?

- These values are derived; one possible reason for a lot of the variance is that we haven't selected the correct summary variable.
  - o This analysis may not sort much out when we take into account sampling errors.
  - o We don't have any model that we can use if we use a different summary variable like INM, unless we use INM-ambient in the analysis (planning to do this for the re-analysis of past data).
- We would want spectral data for future testing?
  - o Once we have that data we still have the problem that have to weight the data over time. For example, NPS likes noise free intervals.
  - o FAA staff want to use the same old metrics as they have been validated, with the exception of low frequency metrics.
- In the past the NPS has talked about L_x values. Recently, we have used time above and time between variables. When you go above "x" level. If you say an LEQ of 46.8 there is nothing to explain the functional consequence

other than referring to the Shultz Curve or Miller Curve. We are completing the historical closure. NPS wasn't managing to a standard and perhaps the NPS wasn't comfortable with automatically accepting the FAA standard. Audibility is simple to explain, besides all the computational difficulties. It is very difficult to communicate the summary variables. I think it is worth examining if we found a variable that was only 80% as effective as LEQ, but easily explained to the public we might want to select it. Nick has suggested time audible,

- o Percent time audible plus how loud it was when it was audible (from discussion yesterday)
- o How loud it is and how long it was there. You can get a picture and develop an intuition.
- o You could plot multiple variables and plot contours. Contours are nice, but not as simple as simple curve.
- o Even experts have trouble sensing and perceiving accurately. Separate the time present and the energy when it is present.
- o Useful to tease out these theories in the lab when time audible at 10%, 20% etc?
- Has there ever been research on combining?
  - o Did a study and the noise and number combination is not that different from Leq. That was done in the 1960s and 70s and finally people dropped analyses of the separate components of noise and just accepted Leq.
- Take away: Continue to explore other options for acoustic summary variables.

Lab Tests

Lab studies could be useful for comparing the elements of metrics that don't yield useful results in the field.

- It is important to gain context as people are trying to do something.
- NASA conducted this type of lab work a long time ago with long rating sessions. They did not continue partly because it was less efficient because and they did not obtain a lot of observations for single individuals. The work did not yield many data points and was very expensive.
- Have investigated how does dB rate and looking at how noise relates to crowding.
- At NPS we have discussed if we need to go to full binaural headset or whether a monaural simulation will recreate conditions and provide the salient results.
- Is it simpler to take the metrics and look for correlation between them?
  - o I always do that, especially for the mediators. Relative Leq correlates greatly with the absolute Leq. I don't worry about have two dimensional components of the dose.

Day 3

Lab Tests (con't)

To what extent can lab research simulate real-world, outdoor studies? This is worth further study

- Look at European examination / directive on noise. They judge rural quality with visual and audio combined. How do people interpret this with respect to sound?
- We could push for a study of visual effects of crowding – multi-sensory studies.
- Parks are not just what you see, it surrounds you. In a lab one can rank order /compare 2 sounds for annoyance. First show picture, than play sound, then show/play together.
  - o Can do full binaural recording, for more accurate spatial reconstruction of sound experience.
- Audio clip evaluation (in the field) appears to be a successful approach. As a strategy, it would be worth trying that first, before trying the lab.
  - o Most aircraft pass-by are 3 – 5 minute event, which is a long play-back.
  - o A lab study could have paid participants, they can tolerate longer intervals.
  - o If the duration of each playback is a question, then conduct fewer, but longer playbacks. Can get into some of the more complex acoustical properties

- o Are we going to get the same % of people to respond with longer playbacks?
- Can we identify a more cost effective method than the lab option?
  - o It is easier to get people to watch a nature film with a "doctored" sound track. People get closer to the experience.
- The implication here is still that brand name dose-response is the gold standard. We need to take a step back and identify whether this is the gold standard. What are the ways we may be concerned about adopting as gold standard
- We want to ID relationship between noise and response. This type of study would compare results in the field vs. results in the lab. In lab can increase sample size. Would lab be appropriately representative of field results? Does lab predict visitor experience in field? There has been resistance to dose-response in NPS.
- What are the limitations of the meter and survey studies (correlate meter to survey)? It could be a lesson learned, now that we have an opportunity to do more.
- Might get same dose response curve in field and lab, but might have different mediating variables.
  - o For a particular mediating variable, don't have control over range in field. Lab overlooks full effect on visitor experience. Is there a different indicator of visitor experience for park policy purposes that we do not get in field studies?
  - o Can you tweak mediators? Are they manageable in the field?
  - o In the site you know the mediating variable, even if you can't manage them. It is a site sensitivity issue. Not just about control, need to be able to identify the mediators on a site. How much sound are the receptors generating on site? Chattering groups, etc. This is an important issue for further study.
- Take-away: Need to study benefits, limitation, and methods of both lab and field, to determine which approach is best to apply.

Cueing visitors to the issue

We want to study the extent to which a visitor's park experience and reaction to sound/noise is affected when a visitor knows they are part of a park survey (they will listen differently than normally).

- It is also common to inform people of the context of the study when asking them to participate. E.g. trampling vegetation off-trail. Cueing visitors can be a worthwhile exercise.
  - o Policy is a form of queuing. Informs people of what "pristine" means.
- How you ask the questions matters. In a sleep study, asking "To what extent does aircraft noise interfere with your sleep?" correlates to aircraft noise. Ask a different question such as, "what is your quality of sleep?", without mentioning the noise source, and then we find a weaker relationship to aircraft noise. There could be a mistaken attribution issue.
- Cueing and environmental process / public meeting. Pilots, of course say did you cue them by asking them about aircraft noise, vs. general experience. We have to ask about aircraft noise specifically to know if it is an issue.
- One option is to provide general and more specific questions in survey. In addition we might try to anchor the visitor's experience with some very positive experiences. For example, we might first ask about where they had previously experienced the greatest solitude and then ask how they rated today's experience. This creates a connection from greatest solitude to today's experience.
- Annoyance and interference measure the extent to which something is bad. Do you also need positive experience measurements to develop policy?
- Instead of a negative series of questions, how about a 2 sentence introduction to the questionnaire about the existence of aircraft in the park (or general park soundscape), then have the questionnaire be general about quality of experience and soundscape, with ratings and doses of positive to negative to choose from.
  - o Go from general questions about the experience to more specific annoyance questions about sources
  - o It is very different for someone to mention aircraft when asked generally about park experience, compared with be asking directly about annoyance from aircraft.

- Take away: There are 3 approaches – totally cued. Quality of experience cued and not cued. In cognitive pretests we might ask for full recall and explanation of what we want you to think about while going through survey.

Agency Summary:

- FAA agrees we deal differently with communities vs. parks. If results show once set of answers conclusive, and the other inclusive, FAA would go with conclusive results.
- NPS would go with the most protective results
- Need to make decisions in coordination with others (diverse backgrounds, experiences, values) in an iterative process with a lot of communication

Group Check-ins:

- Regularly scheduled (perhaps monthly) conference calls.

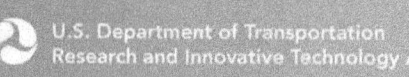

VOLPE center · The National Transportation Systems Center · U.S. Department of Transportation Research and Innovative Technology Administration

The remainder of the day focused on prioritization and sequencing of the research steps, resulting in the following Draft Research Framework:

<u>Dose-Response Research Framework (Workshop Draft)</u>

The paths are not necessarily sequential, but they have links. Tasks in green can be started immediately.

1)	**Data Re-Analysis**
a)	Determine significant combination/combinations of acoustic summary metrics.
b)	Examine visitor-specific local ambient as a mediating factor.
c)	Highlight and eliminate potential mediators in the database (Incorporate additional context-specific site variables). **(6-9 months)**
d)	Develop a statistical tool to determine # sites/parks/visitors needed for new studies.
e)	Examine post-processing of source ID (non-critical path)
f)	Explore machine learning, infinite dose analysis (non-critical path)
g)	Presentation to FAA/NPS of results/research direction (with 3a) – conclusions, implications for future, questions raised. Can we modify dose / control over flights? (1 month after 1c)
2)	**Survey Development**
a)	Develop list of evaluative dimensions / values / experiences / site-mediators (wholesale list) (3-6 mo.)
i)	Literature review , visitor-type focus groups
b)	Evaluate direct/indirect questions of visitor experience with/without cueing. Evaluate comparability with previous dose-response survey data (not required for focus group, evaluative test optimistically 2010, OMB, 18-24 months)
c)	Develop draft survey instrument for review (prerequisite, 2a, 2b 18-24 months)
3)	**NPS Focus Meeting (prerequisites, 2a, conduct in 6 mo.)**
a)	Present and solicit feedback on list of evaluative dimensions / experiential values / site-mediators / site-characterizations / site proto-types, listening exercise
4)	**Site Selection**
a)	Perform campground / interpretive-talk site scoping.
b)	Perform NPS site inventory (manager survey(s)) on needs for noise management information, sound preservation issues (3 months)
c)	Re-visit research Plan. Synthesis of re-analysis, focus groups, site-inventory/scoping to assess relative advantages of sites. (6 mo)
d)	Convene a workgroup/workshop to develop site-specific project schedule (3 mo)
5)	**Methodological development**
a)	Comparative test of field-dose collection methods for dispersed/ wide-area sites. (Dosimeter, Model, Direct measure) (6-9 mo)
b)	Research to answer questions of when/where/how to survey for longer visit durations (>2-4 hours)? Full visit or segmented visit? Develop & test survey. (18-24 mo)
c)	Develop electronic survey instrument (12 mo)
d)	Investigate field audio-playback simulations
e)	Investigate the role of laboratory experiments (TBD, as required)